Praise for *Why God Calls Us to Dangerous Places*

Once again Kate McCord shares a compelling vision of life and ministry on the front lines of human need. By the time you are done reading, you will be reminded of both the triumph and joy of doing God's will, no matter the danger, risk, or cost. If you're not careful, you just might be inspired to pack your bags and go yourself—or join in sending someone else ready to go for Him!

PEGGY FLETCHER
Cofounder, Pioneers

God risked in order to communicate His love. Kate McCord believes we can emulate that compassion by imitating Jesus. May this book challenge us all to obey Him no matter where He calls us.

CHRIS FABRY
Author, radio host

The remaining harvest in God's kingdom is in the hard and dangerous places. God's love compels us to go despite our fears of safety and security. This book offers no gilded promises for those who answer the call, only the remarkable reality of God's presence and power as they minister faithfully in the darkest corners of this earth. It is a must-read for anyone feeling the Spirit-led tug on their heart. Read, take courage, and then go.

PAUL NYQUIST, PhD
President, Moody Bible Institute

The world has become increasingly more difficult and dangerous for those called to share the love and light of Jesus Christ. Kate captures the essence of the challenges facing highly motivated men and women who leave behind material comfort, family, and relational roots to love and heal in Jesus' name. She draws out and helps us understand the deep and abiding love of Jesus and His message of salvation, which motivates and sustains those called to dangerous places.

RICK ALLEN
CEO, MedSend

When it comes to fulfilling the Great Commission of Jesus in our day, the most underserved people on earth reside in very dangerous places. Someone has to have the courage to go there—and Kate McCord is one who did. This book is an amazing firsthand account of one woman who dared to go to Afghanistan and be His light in that darkness. Kate declares, "We go to dangerous places with Jesus and we're never the same."

HANS FINZEL
President of HDLeaders and bestselling auth
Leaders Make **and** *Change Is Like a Slinky*

I strongly recommend this outstanding book. It delicately balances the inevitable high price of taking up our cross daily and following Jesus—wherever He sends us—with the inestimable privileges and eternal rewards of following the most magnificent master in the universe. King Jesus. The lover of our souls.

JOY DAWSON
Youth With A Mission (YWAM)

Here is a refreshing, yet sober look, at dangerous assignments. McCord, a missionary serving for nearly a decade in Afghanistan, speaks from experience as a frontline veteran. During her years in that worn-torn country she has experienced every imaginable danger along with heartbreaking martyrdom of close colleagues. She builds her case for why God calls some to dangerous assignments not on armchair theory but experience laced with biblical reflections.

MARVIN J. NEWELL
Senior vice president, Missio Nexus, author of *A Martyr's Grace*

Kate McCord's talk is born of a faithful walk. She makes a compelling case for followers of Christ entering places of danger with abandon. She offers comfort for those who send and courage for those who go. Her understanding is no dry and dusty theological system divorced from life. This book will disturb, enlighten, and inspire you to follow Christ wherever He leads.

CHARLES W. BECKETT
Senior minister, Woodlawn Christian Church, Knoxville, TN
Father of Cheryl, a 21st-century martyr

One of the biggest lies embraced by the Western church is God loves us so much He would never ask us to do anything difficult, certainly not dangerous. In this richly illustrated and biblically based book, written out of the overflow of life experience, Kate McCord calls us back to a God-centered theology of risk and suffering. It is a much needed and timely message. I highly commend it to you.

STEVE MOORE
Executive director, nexleader, a next generation initiative of ABHE

WHY GOD CALLS US TO DANGEROUS PLACES

KATE MCCORD

MOODY PUBLISHERS

CHICAGO

All Scripture quotations, unless otherwise indicated, are taken from *The Holy Bible, English Standard Version.* Copyright © 2000, 2001 by Crossway Bibles, a division of Good News Publishers. Used by permission. All rights reserved.

Scripture quotations marked NASB are taken from the *New American Standard Bible*®, Copyright © The Lockman Foundation 1960, 1962, 1963, 1968, 1971, 1972, 1973, 1975, 1977, 1995. Used by permission.

Scripture quotations marked NLT are taken from the *Holy Bible, New Living Translation,* copyright © 1996. Used by permission of Tyndale House Publishers, Inc., Wheaton Illinois 60189, U.S.A. All rights reserved.

Scripture quotations marked NIV are taken from the *Holy Bible, New International Version*®. NIV®. Copyright © 1973, 1978, 1984, 2011 by International Bible Society. Used by permission of Zondervan Publishing House. All rights reserved.

Edited by Cheryl Molin
Interior design: Ragont Design
Cover design: Gearbox and Erik M. Peterson
Cover photo of landscape copyright © 2015 by Maximilian Guy McNair MacEwan/ Stocksy/541568. All rights reserved.

Library of Congress Cataloging-in-Publication Data

McCord, Kate.
Why God calls us to dangerous places / Kate McCord.
   pages cm
Includes bibliographical references.
ISBN 978-0-8024-1341-3
 1. Risk taking (Psychology)—Religious aspects—Christianity. 2. Trust in God— Christianity. 3. Suffering—Religious aspects—Christianity. I. Title.
BV4598.15.M33 2015
248.8'6—dc23
                    2015016276

To Debbie, who allowed me to bring
Afghanistan to her screened-in porch.

CONTENTS

INTRODUCTION

The writing of this book brought a flood of memories, tears and joy, humility, and a deep sense of God's astonishing love. I found myself once again grateful for the privilege of walking with Christ in a dangerous place, for the people I've met, and, more than anything else, for the many ways the journey has taken me deeper into the heart of God.

For me, Christ's invitation led to a nine-year journey in Afghanistan, and so my personal experiences and the context from which I asked the question are that very dangerous place. Today, as in the past, Christ calls His people to walk in dangerous places all across the world. The countries are unique, but Christ remains the same.

Each day as I wrote, I prayed for the words God would have me share. I knew He was with me, guiding me, and blessing me with His pleasure.

Somewhere in the middle of the third chapter, I realized that I wanted to invite others to share how the journey with Christ to a dangerous place had affected them. I sent my simple request to a number of people whose journeys I knew. The first to respond was Werner Groenewald, a South African living with his wife and children in Kabul, Afghanistan. Werner's initial response arrived on Friday evening, Kabul time. He wrote, "If I don't get back to you this week, please remind me! I really want to contribute." The next day at 5:37 p.m., Kabul time, Werner sent me his quote. After dark that same evening, the Taliban attacked Werner's home, killing him and his two children.

I've included Werner's words in this book along with the words of many others who shared their thoughts with me over the weeks that followed Werner's and his children's deaths. The words these tender friends have shared are deeply precious to me.

I also realized that I wanted to share the thoughts and reflections of those who have loved those called to a dangerous place. Again, I sent my simple request, this time to family members, friends, and church leaders. Their words are also dear to me, and so I've included many of their quotes.

I've hidden the identities of all workers and family members of workers to protect those who are still walking with God in a dangerous place. I did include Werner's name along with his words at his request.

This book is soaked in Scripture, some passages by reference and others quoted. I've included the references in endnotes. These are some of the truths God has used to speak to my heart as I've sought answers for my own questions. I would encourage you to look up the passages, study them, pray, even read them aloud, and listen for what God would say to you.

I've also included discussion questions at the end of each chapter. Most are meant to be reflective and to facilitate open and honest heart-level conversation. I hope you find them useful.

I love comments and feedback and value your experience, thoughts, and ideas. You can reach me on Facebook at Kate McCord-Storyteller or via my blog at www.storytellerkm.com.

My prayer is that as you read this book, God would take you ever deeper into His astonishing love for you and for all those who live in dangerous places.

Chapter 1

THE QUESTION

"Our very question invites God to reveal His heart to us."

Early on a morning in August 2010, I carried a cup of hot coffee and my laptop onto my friend's screened porch. I'd only been back in the States for a couple of weeks and still bore the deep exhaustion of my previous season in Afghanistan.

I set my coffee and laptop onto the table and breathed my thanks to God: for the porch, the screens that kept it bug free, the cool air, and the dense trees that filtered the morning light. I thought of my friend who was still sleeping upstairs and silently thanked her for welcoming me, once again, into her quiet, peaceful home.

I sat down on a wooden Adirondack chair, sipped my coffee, and logged onto my computer. My computer, such a faithful companion—a battered Toshiba laptop still laced in Afghan dust. It booted slowly and so I sipped my coffee, breathed the morning air, and watched the blessedly dust-free leaves float in the gentle breeze.

Quiet. Peaceful. America.

Still, my body was only slowly uncoiling from the tight, chronic stress of life in a war zone.

The previous year in Afghanistan had been both joyous and exhausting. In the summer of 2009, while I was in the midst of preparing to receive a team of young adults who were exploring overseas work, the Afghan secret police informed me of a specific kidnapping threat. They were sure I was the target. I packed my evacuation bag in a chaotic rush, my insides numb with shock and confusion. The next day, the police discovered that I had not been the target after all, so I returned to my Afghan home.

I continued plans to welcome the team while more threats surfaced. Finally, at around 4:30 in the afternoon, just a few days before the team was meant to arrive, an explosion rocked my house. The concussion struck my ribs with the force of a flat board swung by a strong man. I gasped, caught the wall and my breath, and realized what I had to do.

The team was already on its way, so I traveled to Dubai to meet and tell them, "I'm so sorry. But it's just too dangerous right now for you to come." Confused and disappointed, the team, four young adults, spent a couple of weeks in Dubai and then made their way to Jordan while I returned to my Afghan home.

A month later, I prepared to leave the country for a break.

Once again, I faced a kidnapping threat. This time it wasn't specific, but was instead associated with the road I needed to travel.

How does one pack for a possible kidnapping? I spent hours deciding, un-deciding, re-deciding. Really. How does one pack for a possible kidnapping? Late in the afternoon I gave up, zipped my bag closed, and resigned myself to whatever would happen to me the next day.

That evening, I found a large piece of white board, took out my markers and colored pencils, and went to work. I covered the sheet with pencil-drawn faces, eyes looking straight at me, some full of fear, some resolve. Then, with Magic Marker, I began writing the names of God, first in the backward looping characters of the Dari alphabet, then in the boxier characters of my own English. Khuda Qaderi Mutlack, all-powerful God, Master of the universe, Lover of my soul. I wrote until there was no more space, and, in the writing, began to find peace.

When I finished the board, I wrapped my knees in my arms and started to sing. Over the course of the next several hours, I sang every worship song I knew.

That night, I slept easily and gently. At six o'clock in the morning, I pulled a blue burqa over my head, slipped into Afghan sandals, and sat down in the back seat of an old Russian taxi. In the front, a gray-bearded Pashtun man gave me instructions. "Keep your face covered. Don't let your hands show. When they stop us, look away. Don't let them see your blue eyes through the screen."

Next to him sat a middle-aged, bearded Hazara man with a

small gray turban. "I will tell them you are my wife. There will be many checkpoints. Some will be illegal. Just don't move and please, please, don't say anything."

I sat in the backseat, watching the world through the screen of my burqa. I prayed, sang songs inside my heart, recalled Scriptures, and watched. I had no idea what would happen, and yet I was oddly at peace.

We did stop at checkpoint after checkpoint. At one, men with Kalashnikovs (military assault weapons), some in uniform, some not, questioned us closely. I knew the consequences of being found out; my driver and chaperone would likely be killed, and I would be taken to God knows where. I kept my eyes averted and my heart focused on Jesus. It took us three hours to cross over to safety.

That experience and so many others took their toll.

In the spring of 2010, I planned yet another out-of-country trip. I needed to see a doctor for a test that could not be performed in Afghanistan. I bought a ticket for Wednesday, May 18, 2010, on Pamir Airways.

On Tuesday afternoon, May 17, I packed a small suitcase and made arrangements to travel to the airport the following morning. Just as I finished packing, I received a startling phone call. It began with a gasp. "Thank God." Then followed in a rush of words, "I knew you were going. I couldn't remember what day. Did you hear?"

"Hear what?"

The story that followed took my breath away. The morning

flight, one day before the one I was meant to take, never reached its destination. Instead, the plane crashed into the Salang, the mountains in the middle of Afghanistan. All the passengers and crew were killed.[1]

I missed death by a day, just one day.

I never did make that medical appointment.

The challenges of that season in Afghanistan weren't over. In late May 2010, Afghan television showed a cellphone film of a group of Afghan men praying, worshiping, and being baptized as Christians. Riots swept through the streets of my small town. Once again, I packed my evacuation bag, this time to the staccato rhythm of automatic gunfire and the sounds of men yelling beyond the walls.

I spent the day dressed and ready to go, my scarf around my head and my sandals on my feet. By evening, the rioters had disbanded and an uneasy calm settled over the city. The next day, Friday, the day of afternoon prayers, I took my evacuation bag and sought refuge in a nearby foreign military base.

I was grateful when the mullahs[2] called for calm and our town returned to normal. By evening, I was once again back in my Afghan home.

These things take their toll.

Sometime in early July, a neighbor called me to his house. I drank tea with him and his wife and children. We talked about floods and orchards and crops and I wondered why he had requested my presence. Eventually, he got to his point.

Men, outsiders, perhaps from Kabul, had come to our neighborhood mosque. They had a simple request: throw rockets at the foreign woman.

I kept my calm. "What did the men in the mosque decide?"

"They decided they will watch you."

So they did. They talked to my staff, the beneficiaries of my projects, my neighbors, and the shopkeepers on the corners. And they watched me. Men stood in groups and watched me walk out of my house. They watched the gates I disappeared through and waited for me to return. They talked among themselves: assessing, evaluating, deciding.

The stress takes its toll.

Finally, at the end of July 2010, I packed my things and returned to America. I desperately needed a break. I needed peace. I needed to breathe. That morning I sat with my morning coffee and laptop on my friend's screened-in porch and watched the leaves gently float in the morning breeze. When my laptop booted, I clicked onto email.

I think I stopped breathing. I know my limbs went cold. I read all the message headers at the same time. I couldn't move. I saw names of senders: coworkers and friends from my town in Afghanistan, friends from Kabul, others who normally lived in Afghanistan but were now in England, Canada, or Seattle. I saw their names and felt a wail rise up from within the pit of my stomach. And yet, I had no breath. My cry was trapped—cold, hard, and fierce.

I began clicking on the messages and slowly the story took shape. A team of foreign medical workers had been executed in the mountains of northern Afghanistan.[3]

My mind spun. Faces of friends floated into focus, and yet I didn't know who was on that team. I searched the Internet for names, but the release of information was slow. I returned to the emails and pieced the stories together. I recognized one and then another and then another member of that team.

I don't remember what happened after that. The next few days are lost to me. I do remember that at some point that morning my friend, whose house I was staying in, awakened. She walked out onto the porch, took one look at me, and began to cry. I don't know what she saw in my face, but it was enough to tell her that something had gone terribly wrong.

BOTH WE WHO GO, and those who love those who go, face the deep evil in the world and turn to God with all our human fragility. We ask the question: why does God call us to dangerous places? Our very question invites God to reveal His heart to us.

I remember trying to explain what little I knew and at the same time wishing for all the world that we were not having this conversation on her cool, peaceful porch. I knew that once again I had brought violence and loss into the life of someone whose heart went to Afghanistan because it went with me.

I wanted to protect her, to shield her from the loss and the pain and the fear. I wanted her to be like other Americans for whom Afghanistan is just a news report. But it was too late. She'd already seen the pictures of my Afghan friends. She'd heard their voices on audio files I'd recorded. And more than anything else, she'd listened to my stories. She'd heard my voice and seen my eyes when I talked about people I had come to know and love so deeply.

For my friend, Afghanistan was and will always be a place full of precious and beautiful human beings and also a place of devastating violence. Although she never stepped down from a plane at Kabul airport, she, like the friends and families of all of us who go to a dangerous place, had certainly been there. The losses I experienced, she experienced with me.

So on that August morning, my friend sat down on an Adirondack chair in a tree-enclosed porch in the middle of America and wept for a group of fragile human beings who had been brutally executed in the mountains of Afghanistan, and for their friends and families who would never be the same.

Since that August day, other aid workers have been killed or kidnapped in Afghanistan. The names and stories of some have been posted on the Internet. Most, especially those who were kidnapped, held hostage, and later freed will remain forever nameless except to those who know and love them.

None of us will ever be the same. The trauma many of us have experienced is real. It's shaped us, marked, and transformed us.

We ask our question from the experiences of living in places of chronic stress, sporadic trauma, and brutal martyrdom. Both we who go, and those who love those who go, face the deep evil in the world and turn to God with all our human fragility. We ask the question: why does God call us to dangerous places?

Our very question invites God to reveal His heart to us.

As I write these words, I'm remembering a European husband and father who spent a month chained to an Afghan man. Hostages. I'm thinking about his wife and children who spent that same month trying to breathe. I know of a father who buried his daughter in the Afghan dust and who somehow found the grace to forgive those who had taken her from him. I think of a woman who remembers her martyred friends every time she eats pancakes because that was something they'd done together.

I'm writing, also, for the mothers and fathers who wake up in the morning and check the news just to make sure their children are still alive; and grandmothers who swallow their fear, Skype with their grandchildren, and ache to have them home.

I'm writing for the workers who come home shattered, lost, and confused; and the friends, families, and church communities who struggle to receive them.

My question isn't limited to Afghanistan, but encompasses all the dangerous places—places where people go because Christ calls them to do so.

A young mother loses her husband to dengue fever in southeast Asia. A family is plucked from a roof in Chad. Another family is lost in Yemen. The children turn up, but the parents are never found. A college student with a heart for inner-city ministry is brutally assaulted and killed. Black leather–coated men enter a house in Central Asia and carry a husband away. Days later he's returned, but neither he nor his wife will ever be the same.

That's the thing; we're never the same. We go to dangerous places with Jesus, and we're never the same.

Somewhere along the journey, we each look into the face of darkness and ask a frightening question: why does God call His beloved children to such a dangerous place?

It's a fair question, necessary, personal. And we're not the first to ask it.

Before us, generations of Christian evangelists, doctors, teachers, and aid workers followed Christ to Japan, Ghana, Fiji, Palestine, and a host of other dangerous locations. They faced disease, hunger, war, and even cannibalism and crucifixion. Some died, some were killed, and some returned home, their mental and physical health broken.

Nor are any of us giants. We are not Christian Navy SEALs, the toughest, most committed, most hard-core followers of Christ. Instead, we are completely human.

We are idealistic young men and women hoping to bring light and love into the world. We are occupational therapists who teach local mothers how to help their children afflicted with cerebral palsy. We are art therapists who help Serbian children make sense of the war they've experienced. We are seasoned aid workers feeding the hungry in Syrian refugee camps. We are retirees who have raised our children and answered the call to train medical personnel in West Africa.

We are doctors and lawyers, dancers and writers, project managers, technologists, and linguists. We are flesh and blood. Fragile. Hopeful, sometimes frightened, always human.

And those who send us are just like us: sisters, brothers, mothers, fathers, friends, grandparents. Some of us go to church and raise our hands. Some of us sing the liturgy and kneel before the Communion rail. We read NIV Bibles, KJV, NASB, ESV, and any of a dozen other translations. We attend denominational churches, house churches, and independent churches.

WE FACE SQUARELY and honestly what it means to follow Christ into a world that does not know Him. As we do so, we find answers that move beyond romance and excitement. We find purpose, comfort, and the peace that Christ offers us—a peace beyond even the most horrific circumstances. We find the heart of God.

We are wealthy and poor, white, Asian, African American, Hispanic. We are married and single, men and women, old and young.

The thing we all hold in common is that we love Jesus and we've walked with Him into a dangerous place.

For some of us the journey has been shattering. It's important to say that. It's important to recognize that when we talk about walking with Christ into a dangerous place, we're talking about pain, fear, and loss. We're talking about stress, trauma, secondary trauma, and posttraumatic stress. Yet we go and count it a privilege to do so.

In our experience, we face squarely and honestly what it means to follow Christ into a world that does not know Him. As we do so, we find answers that move beyond romance and excitement. We find purpose, comfort, and the peace that Christ offers us—a peace beyond even the most horrific circumstances. We find the heart of God.

As I write, my shoulders are tense and my breath shallow, and yet I sense holiness. There's something sacred in the journey—something sacred for all of us. Something none of us would trade for anything in the world.

In the fall of 2012, I took a train from Germany into Holland. I had made arrangements to visit dear friends from Afghanistan. For the sake of sharing the story, I'll change their names.

I'd not seen Lars, Noa, and their children since Lars's kidnapping; a crisis event that cost all of us dearly. I'd been planning the visit for some time and was sure I was ready, but I wasn't.

I arrived at the station early and decided on a short walk before our meeting. It didn't take me long to start crying. I can't tell you why I was crying, only that I was and I couldn't stop. I must have been a sight, a solitary woman dragging a suitcase down a midday street, sobbing. Strangers passed by and looked away.

Eventually, I gathered my breath and returned to the train station. I found Noa waiting for me. The joy of seeing her and the pain of our shared experience nearly swept my legs from beneath me.

Later that evening the three of us—Lars, Noa, and I—sat together, breathed, and shared our stories. Noa talked about shock, fear, and deep sadness. Lars described his chains and helplessness. I spoke of shock and numbness.

If our conversation had stayed there, I think we would have drowned. Instead, I noticed something subtle but deep. We each shared glimpses, soft touches of grace. We reflected on how God had prepared us before the crisis to walk through it. We talked about the different ways He had been with each of us through the long season of Lars's captivity. We reflected on the gentleness with which He had held us when the kidnapping was over and we each lay wounded, exhausted, and confused in His arms.

We spoke these things through tears and trembling words. In doing so, we touched threads of Christ's presence woven through a dense and traumatic tapestry. It was not a conversation of exultant victory. There was no celebratory glory, but there was certainly glory.

In the midst of our pain-filled conversation, I recognized that we were sitting in the sacred, the holy. We had brushed against the eternal, transcendent God. Our trauma, sorrow, and grief were interwoven with grace, love, and even, though it's impossible to explain, joy.

I know as I write this that these are mysteries more profound than the words I choose to articulate them. I also know that I am grateful for having experienced Christ so deeply. In a very intense way, we shared both in Christ's suffering and His resurrection, and I am awed in the complete sense of that word.

Shortly after my trip to Holland, I found myself at church in America. We were celebrating Communion and the worship band was playing a simple, familiar song taken from Psalm 27:4:

> One thing have I asked of the LORD,
> that will I seek after:
> that I may dwell in the house of the LORD
> all the days of my life,
> to gaze upon the beauty of the LORD
> and to inquire in his temple.

Before I went to Afghanistan, I had thought God's presence was an escape from the chaos and pain of the world, and I longed to be in that place of perfect peace, love, and joy. But that Sunday morning, as we sang and shared the broken bread and cup, I realized I had indeed seen the beauty of the Lord. I had seen God's sorrow and God's joy, God's suffering and God's celebration.

That was not the vision I wanted and yet I was transfixed, held in place by a force I could not define. Part of me wanted to shout, "No! This is not what I signed up for. This is not what I want." I ached to push my way out of the pew and flee God's terrible beauty, and yet I couldn't move. I was captivated by a God who loves completely, not in denial but rather in embrace—a God who, in the place of suffering, both suffers and loves.

This book is my humble attempt to explore what it means to know this God who suffers and loves and invites His fragile children into life with Him.

DISCUSSION GUIDE

Chapter 1: The Question

Please take time to reflect on what you have read. You can use the space provided, or better yet, use a separate journal to go deeper into the Scriptures and truths that are written.

1. How do you think God views the suffering of some of His people?

2. Can you imagine following Christ even if the journey includes suffering and loss?

3. Consider Psalm 27:4. Write out the verse. What do you desire most from the Lord?

4. For what or for whom do you sense God consistently calling your attention, care, or concern?

5. What are the gifts, talents, and abilities that God
    has given to you in this season? Can you offer them
    back to Him?

6. Are you willing to follow Christ wherever He leads?

Chapter 2

MY STORY

*"They had no idea what they were
walking into, but they ached to go."*

My own journey with Jesus to a dangerous place began in a
quiet season of my life.

In 2000, I was working as a business process consultant in
global biopharmaceutics. I had a great job, worked with a wonderful group of people, owned a lovely house, and drove a convert-
ible. I was a member of my church and the chair of our missions
committee.

Life was good.

I could've coasted; I might have held on to God's blessings
and refrained from seeking anything more. But God was stirring
a deeper hunger within me, and I responded with a desire for
more of Him. I had no idea what that might mean in my life. All
I knew was that God was calling me to a renewed consecration,
to give back to Him all He had placed in my hands.

I recall one Sunday evening in particular. I was at prayer meeting at my church and the worship band was playing softly. I had just returned from a business trip to Europe and was still wearing my suit and black dress shoes. I remember slipping off my shoes, pulling my laptop from my backpack, kneeling on the carpet at the foot of the cross, and placing my laptop on the floor in front of me.

I prayed. I offered God my laptop, and in doing so offered Him my career, my income, and my 401(k). I didn't realize it, but I was also offering God my identity and my purpose. I understood the holiness of my actions but couldn't even begin to guess at where such consecration might lead me. I only knew that I didn't want to coast, that I wanted to follow Christ no matter where He led.

That night, I did not ask God for a mission. I'd not even begun to think about Afghanistan and wasn't actively looking for some grand adventure or even a new journey for my life. I would've been quite satisfied to pick up my laptop and keep working in the corporate world for the rest of my working life. If such had been my course, I believe I would've followed it with the rich and full satisfaction of knowing I was exactly where God wanted me.

When I prayed that evening, I didn't see any visions nor did I hear any words. I simply knew the sweet peace of releasing a very significant part of my life to my God.

By the end of that year, everything had started to change.

The first hint of a new journey came in the form of a book

I picked up at the airport in Copenhagen. It was a travel book about Afghanistan called *An Unexpected Light: Travels in Afghanistan*[1] by Jason Elliot. I chose it because I thought it would be interesting, not because I wanted my world rocked. By the time I landed in the United States, I was captivated.

I woke up the next day, connected to the Internet, and began reading everything I could find about Afghanistan. I read news articles, ordered books, and watched films. The stories and pictures drove me, day after day, to my knees. Afghanistan haunted me.

In January 2001, I sat in a friend's living room, surrounded by the members of my small group. We had our coffee and our trays of treats and had moved into a time of sharing our prayer requests.

I spoke tentatively. "I believe God is calling me to Afghanistan."

Shock. Denial. "No, He's not."

In those days, the Taliban ruled the country and what few reports we saw were full of horror and oppression. How could God possibly call anyone there?

I knew my friends loved me. They saw both my joy and my fragility. They also saw Afghanistan, albeit from a distance. They knew about the Taliban and oppression and violence. They couldn't see me in that dangerous place, and they didn't want to.

That evening, I understood my friends' reactions and tucked the dream back into my pocket. I knew that if God was calling me, Afghanistan would continue to grow in my heart.

Over the course of the next months, I kept praying, watching, and waiting.

On September 11, 2001, I inhaled the horror of the day's trauma, looked out the window of the office I was standing in, and knew with absolute certainty that I would go to Afghanistan.

I was no rescuer. No superstar. No great white hope. I just knew that Christ had been calling me, inviting me to walk with Him in Afghanistan, and soon, the door would open to go.

When I returned to my small group and again said, "I believe God is calling me to Afghanistan," my friends, trembling and frightened, agreed. That evening and on many subsequent evenings, brothers and sisters in Christ gathered around me to pray for my journey. Some prayed with strength and courage, full of optimistic expectation. Others prayed with sadness yet resolve. Some tried to talk me out of it, and some chose to walk with me through it. Many of those friends are still with me, and together we have walked with Christ in a dangerous land.

None of us knew where the journey would take us, nor how much it would cost us, nor how it would transform us. Still, we went.

Over the years, I've looked into Scripture to make sense out of the sorrow and joy I've experienced. The story of James and John and their father, Zebedee, drew my attention.

I imagine the three of them, along with their coworkers, mending their nets.[2] I love that little phrase, "mending their nets." They were working, minding their own business, living their lives. They were taking care of their families, doing the good and right.

I've never mended nets, but I've spent a lot of time writing reports, doing emails, and facilitating meetings—minding my own business, living my life. And here comes Jesus with a book and a burden. Come, follow Me to Afghanistan.

Except, with James and John the invitation came slightly differently. I see Jesus walking along the beach. Peter and Andrew are already with Him and perhaps there are others we don't know about. This little group walks up the beach toward Zebedee, a father, and his sons, James and John, and their hired men.

I doubt if we have the full conversation, but we have enough. Jesus, surrounded by Peter and Andrew and perhaps others, calls out to James and John as He had called to them, "Follow Me."[3]

The Scripture says that immediately James and John left their father and followed Jesus,[4] but I want to pause here in the space of time between the invitation and the departure.

I imagine James and John, two young men working side by side with their father. I imagine they saw something deeply significant in the man, Jesus, who stood on the shore and invited them to go with Him. I'm sure something in them knew, just knew that following Jesus was their destiny.

But did they have any idea where they were going, what they would experience along the way, or how it would change them? I don't think so.

In the beginning of my own journey with Jesus to a dangerous place, I had hundreds of questions. My friends and family had questions too. I'm sure James, John, and their father had their own questions.

Could we recast the story into something that might appeal to our twenty-first-century Western sensibilities? Jesus stands on the shore with Peter and Andrew and perhaps a few others. He offers His invitation.

James and John look up from their nets. "Sure, but what's Your vision?"

Jesus smiles. "Let Me tell you about the road ahead, about what you will experience if you follow Me. You'll see the most astonishing things. The blind will see, the lame walk, even the dead will return to life."

The young men grow excited. Their father hesitates. The story is too good to be true.

Jesus continues. "You'll have a wonderful time. You will love and be loved. You'll learn and grow and experience so much. Plus, you'll make a lasting difference in the world."

The young men leap off the boat.

Zebedee calls his sons back. "Wait a minute. Where's the catch? These are difficult times. Following a rogue preacher has consequences. What's the hitch?"

Jesus nods. "Yes. These are difficult times. I'm sorry, young men, but there are other things you will experience, too. People will hate us. They'll curse us and try to kill us. For a while, they won't succeed, but eventually, they will kill Me, brutally, and one of you will watch."

James and John freeze in their tracks.

Zebedee cries out, "I knew it!"

Jesus continues, "Oh, and one of you will also be killed."

"No," Zebedee shouts. "My sons! I forbid it."

And perhaps, James and John also hesitate. The brothers study each other's faces. No, the invitation doesn't sound at all appealing.

And yet, we know that many times during their journey with Jesus, both James and John did have the opportunity to walk away, but neither did. We know that John stood at the foot of the cross and watched his beloved Companion die a hideous death. We know that James, his brother, was put to death.

In the shadow of such trauma, John summed up his experience with Jesus: "And the Word became flesh and dwelt among us, and we have seen his glory, glory as of the only Son from the Father, full of grace and truth."[5] Surely, he hadn't forgotten the violence and humiliation of the cross, and yet he spoke of glory, grace, and truth.

When John reflected on how the journey had affected him, he wrote, "See what kind of love the Father has given to us, that we should be called children of God; and so we are."[6]

John, who had no idea what this Jesus on the beach was calling him into, left his father, his career, and his home to follow the Jesus he saw and heard that day. And later, much later, after the miracles and the teachings, after the Last Supper, the garden and the cross, after he encountered the resurrected Lord and saw Him ascend, after he buried his brother, he still wrote, "And this is eternal life, that they know you the only true God, and Jesus

Christ whom you [God] have sent."[7]

There's no way young John and James could have understood the journey that lay ahead of them. No way they could've heard the warnings of the traumas they would face and believe that later, they would use words like *glory, grace, truth, eternal life,* and *children of God.* There's no way, their father's net still in their hands, they could have comprehended a transformation so deep for which and from which they would give their lives.

No. Young James and John encountered a very human Jesus on the beach that day. They heard His voice, felt the *yes* rise within them, and they followed Him. They had no idea what they were walking into, but they ached to go.

Perhaps you can see why their story resonates so much within me. I was a business-process consultant in global biopharmaceutics. Jesus invited me to walk with Him in Afghanistan, and everything within me said *yes.* And now, looking back, well aware of the beauty and brutality, I wouldn't trade it for anything in the world.

The story the Gospel offers us is not just about Jesus, James, and John. There's another person present on the beach that day: Zebedee, a father.

Over the years I've thought quite a bit about this man. He was a fisherman, a father, and a husband. Perhaps he also had daughters, some married, some still at home. Perhaps he had grandchildren.

He owned a boat and had servants or hired men. And so,

he was a provider, for the men who worked for him and for his family.

I imagine he was a good man, a man who loved his sons. He likely enjoyed their presence, day in and day out, both at work and at home. He undoubtedly relied upon them, their strength, skill, and commitment. His fishing business was a family operation.

What did he think and feel when Jesus, the itinerant preacher from Nazareth, appeared on the shore and invited his sons to leave him? How did he react?

The Scripture says nothing more of the departure except that it happened. And yet there are things I've chosen to believe.

I believe that Zebedee loved his sons. I imagine his heart ached for his own loss when he watched them walk away. Every day, when he went out on his boat with his hired men, he experienced anew his sons' absence. Every morning and evening when he sat at table with his family, he saw the places his sons previously occupied as empty and silent.

Perhaps it was Zebedee who sent his wife, Salome, to follow the itinerant preacher and keep track of their sons while he himself kept the family business going. Perhaps he placed some of his earnings into his wife's hands to provide for their sons and the traveling band.

Did Salome return home with news of what she had seen and heard? Did the two, father and mother, sit around their table, talk, worry, and pray like so many other parents of children who walk with Jesus in a dangerous place do?

If Zebedee lived, he certainly would have followed the story of Jesus: the itinerant preacher, the challenging prophet, the healer and miracle worker, the subversive revolutionary, the prisoner—and finally the martyr.

Perhaps, as the lives of his sons unfolded, he had moments of anger, at his sons for leaving and at God for taking them. Perhaps he felt moments of deep pride that his sons could be counted among the great man's followers. I imagine he knew times of terrible fear as news of the arrest and crucifixion reached him.

When Salome returned home, shattered by the trauma and transformed by the resurrection, did Zebedee receive her in the fullness of her story?

And then, later, there must've been deep grief when his son James was brutally killed and his son John was still in harm's way.

I pause to consider Zebedee because I've known fathers who've watched their sons and daughters follow Jesus into dangerous places. Each has his own way of making the journey. Some push the whole experience aside and focus on the day-to-day requirements of their careers. Some gather with others, wring their hands, and pray fervently. Some follow the news and read everything they can find about the places their children have gone. Some get on airplanes and visit their sons or daughters on the field.

The point is, no matter how these fathers react, they are part of the story. The journeys of their children are also their journeys. Each experiences it in a unique way, but they all walk it.

And then there is the mother of James and John, Salome.

She's not present on the beach when Jesus walks up and invites her sons to follow Him. I imagine she's back at home, perhaps preparing the next meal. Does she hear the news from her husband, Zebedee, or from someone else? "They've gone." What emotions sweep through her at that moment, at what might feel like the loss of her beloved sons?

Salome is not silent in Scripture. We see her again and again: following Jesus, interceding for her sons,[8] standing at the foot of the cross,[9] and even witnessing the resurrection.[10] We don't know if she came and went, if she spent most of her time with Jesus and her sons or with her husband in their fishing village. All we know is that she, too, is in the story, a mother, well aware of both the beauty and brutality of her sons' journey.

Before I went to Afghanistan, I didn't really think much about Zebedee and Salome. I just didn't consider that when Jesus called James and John, He called their parents too.

Since then, I've listened to the stories and voices of fathers and mothers whose grown daughters and sons were living in the shadow of warring factions in Afghanistan. I've heard their fear, their deep pride, and their churning questions. I've looked into their eyes and held their trembling hands. I've felt their pain.

These are men and women of deep faith. Mothers who held their newborn infants before the Lord and said, "Father, I commit my child to You." These are parents who taught their children to live with integrity and purpose. These are men and women of strong, solid faith who rejoice in their children's journey with

Jesus. They are also fragile human beings assailed by very real doubts and fears.

In the first century and much of the world today, most close relationships were bound in the family, both the nuclear and extended. Today, for many of us, our closest relationships include friends with whom we share our lives. And here was another chance for me to learn.

I remember telling my closest friend, a woman with whom I'd shared a deep friendship for more than twenty years, that God was calling me to Afghanistan. Her reaction was both sweet and revealing.

"How do you know?" she asked.

I told her my story and she said simply, "Ask again." She was sure I had misunderstood, or at least she hoped I had.

Later that day, we drove to a store to pick up something I needed. It was time for me to buy a new pair of glasses, and I wanted her to help me choose the frames. We entered the store and sat down at a table across from a young woman with dark brown eyes, nearly black hair, and skin the color of wheat. I placed my prescription on the desk, and the woman began explaining options to me. It was then that I noticed her accent. It wasn't strong, but definitely present. "Excuse me, but where you from?"

The woman sat up straight in her chair and looked from me to my friend and then back to me. She seemed concerned.

"Really, I'm curious. I hear a little bit of an accent. Where are you from?"

The woman relaxed. "Actually, I moved here when I was a little girl, but I'm originally from Kabul, Afghanistan."

I beamed, excited at the opportunity to speak with an Afghan. My friend fled the store. I took my prescription and excused myself from the young woman. I found my friend sitting in the driver seat of her car, sobbing. That brief and unexpected exchange had confirmed for her what she'd hoped wasn't true—that God was calling her closest friend to Afghanistan.

JESUS WALKED DOWN the beach, saw two young men, James and John, and invited them to follow Him. In doing so, they walked with Jesus through beauty and brutality. Long before they reached the end of their lives, they had chosen to follow Jesus no matter where the journey led them.

Each year when I returned from Afghanistan, I spent time at my friend's house. We sat on her screened-in porch, drank coffee, and shared our stories. She learned that I would return exhausted, unable to make simple decisions, and desperately in need of beauty, quiet, and peace. She also learned that I would bring with me hilarious adventures, joy-filled experiences, and terrifying accounts. All of these we shared.

We also shared the heartbreaking events that reached me via email, cellphone, and Skype: a desperately ill housemate fighting for her life in a military field hospital, a kidnapped friend held hostage beyond our reach, a group of fellow workers killed in the mountains. And more. Always, and still more.

Jesus walked down the beach, saw two young men, James

and John, and invited them to follow Him. In doing so, they walked with Jesus through beauty and brutality. They were transformed along the way. Long before they reached the end of their lives, they had chosen to follow Jesus no matter where the journey led them.

They were also the sons of Zebedee and Salome, a man and woman whose lives were transformed through their children's journey. They count, too—and with them, every mother, father, sibling, cousin, friend, child, and grandparent of those whom Jesus calls to walk with Him in a dangerous place.

All of us, the whole community of fragile human beings who have been touched by this journey, peer into the mystery and struggle to understand. And we must, if we are to grow through our experience and the experiences of others.

For me, one of the first and most important realizations as I walked with Christ in a dangerous place is how much He loves the people who live in such places.

DISCUSSION GUIDE

Chapter 2: My Story

1. Consider Mark 1:19–20. How did Christ first call you to Him?

2. What does it mean to you and your sense of yourself to be God's child?

3. What hinders you now or has hindered you in the past from giving your all to Christ? Can you offer those things to Him?

4. Read John 1:14. Write it out and read it aloud. How would you describe Jesus to someone who's never met Him?

5. Think about the quote from this chapter: "James and John . . . walked with Jesus through beauty and brutality. They were transformed along the way. Long before they reached the end of their lives, they had chosen to follow Jesus no matter where the journey led them." Has this been true in your own journey?

Chapter 3

HOW DEEP THE FATHER'S LOVE

"God calls us to dangerous places because He loves people who live in dangerous places."

Many times during my journey in Afghanistan I loved both the country and its people. Other times, sadly, I didn't. Some days I couldn't stand Afghans. My friends and I would say, "I'm having an 'I hate Afghanistan' day." Those were the days when the dark brutality blinded our eyes to God's ever-present love.

I remember one such day quite clearly. I'd been visiting a group of women in one of the neighborhoods. As was so often the case, my Afghan women friends shared their stories of brutal, painful experiences. That day, one of the women told me of a young cousin who'd been seized by a warlord and given to his soldiers. Six weeks later, the girl returned home, but her mind was shattered.

After our tea and conversation, I walked out into the brilliant sunlight with outrage in my heart. That was my mental state when I flagged down a gray-bearded driver in a beat-up taxi. I believe I despised him before I ever entered his vehicle.

But something within me changed as we bounced down the road, some shift in my own internal attitude. I can't say how that happened, but I'm sure it didn't come from me.

By instinct and practice, I engaged the driver in conversation. It was my habit, my effort to ensure that strangers recognized me as human and a guest in their country.

At first, our conversation proceeded normally. "How are you? How is your family? Where are you from?"

The taxi driver asked me who I was and what I was doing in his country. I explained that I was an NGO worker (working for a nongovernmental organization) and told him about some of my projects.

He asked me why I would come to such a horrible place when I could very easily stay in America.

I told him that Afghans were my neighbors and that God calls me to love my neighbors. Despite my words, there was little love in my heart.

Our conversation shifted. When I studied the man's face in the rearview mirror, I saw something that looked like deep sadness and regret. It occurred to me that he had been *mujahedin*, a warrior in one of Afghanistan's many wars. I wondered if he had done some terribly bad thing, something he carried like a desecrated corpse in his arms.

I don't know how I recognized these things, but I did. Call it a word of knowledge or just a moment of insight, it doesn't matter. The point is, I saw the man.

At first, I had no compassion—just outrage. Had he been one of the soldiers who had so brutally violated my friend's young cousin? I wanted to know.

But slowly, I recognized that this gray-bearded driver with his bushy eyebrows and deeply lined face was also a wounded human being. I spoke my question gently. "You were mujahedin, weren't you?"

The man's shoulders slumped, but he didn't meet my eyes in the rearview mirror.

"God can forgive you, you know." I was surprised at my own words, not because I didn't believe them, but rather because I didn't want to share them. The man still didn't meet my glance. I asked him again. "You were mujahedin, weren't you?"

He slid down in the front seat.

I watched the sadness spread and deepen across his face.

He shook his head. "No. There are things God cannot forgive."

I knew the Afghan teachings. If a man kills another man, he must be forgiven by the relatives of the man he killed before Allah can forgive him. If a man rapes a woman, he must be forgiven by her father, her husband, or her son before Allah can wash his guilt away. My horror at the man's crime spread through my body. I didn't know of any other sins for which a Muslim man could not find forgiveness in God. And yet, I knew that this

man, no matter what his crime, could indeed find forgiveness in
God in Christ. I knew that he didn't have to carry the weight of
guilt and shame that so obviously marked him.

This time, I didn't ask him but simply stated, "You were
mujahedin."

He nodded his assent, still avoiding my gaze in the mirror.

We neared my house so I spoke quickly. "God can forgive
you." I told him about Jesus carrying our sin and punishment on
the cross. I explained repentance and confession.

We pulled up at the gate outside of my house. I stepped
onto the Afghan street and dropped the fare onto the front seat.

Finally, he met my eyes.

I nodded. "Brother. God can forgive you."

He looked down at his hands resting on the steering wheel
and sighed.

I closed the door and turned away. In that moment, stepping
across the refuse-filled culvert that separated my house from the
street, I breathed the holy. I knew that something sacred had just
happened and that I had been present.

The driver pulled his vehicle away and rumbled down the
street. I had no idea how my words would affect him, what he
would do with them, what peace he would or would not find.
I only knew that that day, in that beat-up old taxi, Christ had
touched a man and I had seen it.

Why does God call us to dangerous places? To places
where men pick up Kalashnikovs and follow warlords into rape,
murder, and theft?

The first answer is difficult for me to accept. It violates my desire for justice.

I had entered that man's taxi deeply disturbed by the story I'd just heard from my Afghan women friends. Of course, sitting in my friends' room, drinking tea, and looking into the faces of women who had seen so much trauma had affected me. Of course their stories had stirred both compassion and outrage. I saw them as victims—as weak and vulnerable women who'd been caught up in horrific violence.

There was no doubt in my mind that the God of the universe who wrapped Himself in the darkness of a young woman's womb and entered our world, small and vulnerable, absolutely loved those Afghan women who had suffered so much.

Why did God call me to Afghanistan, to such a dangerous place full of so many heartbreaking stories? The answer seemed clear: because God loves the weak and vulnerable of Afghanistan. Because God loves the girl kidnapped by the warlord and passed around among his soldiers. Because He loves the women who received that girl home again and saw the devastation of what had happened to her. Because God loves the women who shared their tea with me and told me their stories.

GOD DOESN'T JUST LOVE the historically few first-century people of Jerusalem, Galilee, and points in between. God also loves the twenty-first-century people of Afghanistan, Iraq, and Somalia.

That part was easy.

But what about the driver? What about the gray-bearded man with the bushy eyebrows who carried the weight of some hideous guilt like a corpse he could find no place to bury? Does God love him?

And of course, I knew the answer.

Jesus stood before those who welcomed Him, those who studied Him, and those who hated Him. He stood before those who had no idea who He was. He opened His hands to all who were thirsty because He knew that only He could satisfy the depth of our thirst.[1]

And He sat in a taxi with an angry foreign woman and a weary Afghan man. He saw the weight the man bore and had the same compassion He felt as He looked out over Jerusalem and wept.[2] The same compassion He experienced when He stood at a tomb beside an angry sister.[3] The same compassion that articulated its desire in an invitation: "Come to me, all who labor and are heavy laden, and I will give you rest."[4]

Jesus calls us to dangerous places because He loves people who live in dangerous places. He loves the perpetrators of violence and the victims of violence. He loves the children and the old, the men and the women, the rich and the poor.

God doesn't just love the historically few first-century people of Jerusalem, Galilee, and points in between. God also loves the twenty-first-century people of Afghanistan, Iraq, and Somalia.

For me, holding God's love for the mujahedin fighter–turned–taxi driver beside His love for the girl so horrifically violated is nearly impossible. And yet, such is God's heart and, therefore, His invitation.

One conversation, in particular, helped me find my way.

On a late fall afternoon in Afghanistan, I sat down with a dear friend to drink tea and share stories. I'll call her Arzesh, although that's not her real name.

Arzesh told me with tears in her eyes that she was once again pregnant. She'd already delivered six live children and lost two others. The idea of having another child, another mouth to feed, overwhelmed her. She was grateful that her husband had finally found work, but his pay was low and the family was still living, hand to mouth, in a refugee camp.

Years earlier, they'd lost their comfortable life when the mujahedin buried their Kabul neighborhood in rubble. They'd fled to the north with nothing but their children in their arms. After that earth-shattering flight, Arzesh's husband fell into despair. For many years, he found his peace in opium and idleness. As a consequence, the family suffered further. One daughter was sold to pay a debt. Another daughter was promised for yet another debt.

A few months earlier, Arzesh's husband broke free of the opium and found work, but it still wasn't enough. They owned nothing and their debts were crushing.

And now, there was another child.

I didn't know what to say as my friend gazed through the glass-less window of her small mud house. I simply sat with her and allowed my own tears to fall. Eventually, I asked if I could pray and Arzesh agreed. The two of us lifted our hands and entreated the only One who could help us. I watched as a small measure of peace passed over Arzesh's face. Still, I knew it wasn't enough.

When Arzesh settled down, she filled my teacup and opened a small book of Psalms. We'd been reading them together and finding solace, guidance, and encouragement in the ancient text.

I suggested we read Psalm 139 and hoped the words would strengthen her heart. I had no agenda or lesson plan, only a simple trust in God and His truth.

We read the entire Psalm together, alternating lines. Arzesh read the dense poetry beautifully. I stumbled along but found my way. When we finished, she sighed and returned her gaze to the window.

"Let's read it again."

And so we did, several times over.

After the third reading, I asked her what she liked about it. She had noticed several things but focused first on God's presence with her throughout her life. She talked about the first time she saw her husband and how happy she had been that he had come for her. In those days, he was a university student, handsome, strong, and kind. She adored him. "Was God there? Did He see us?"

We read part of the text again. "You know when I sit down and when I rise up; you discern my thoughts from afar. You search out my path and my lying down and are acquainted with all my ways."[5]

The reality that God was with her—in the university classroom, in her home when her future husband came to negotiate for her hand, in her house when her first children were born, on the road after the mujahedin destroyed her neighborhood—washed over her memories like a scented balm cooling sunburned skin.

We talked about her husband's long addiction to opium and the loss of her daughter to strangers. And again we read the passage. One verse in particular wrapped its gentle truth around her: "If I say, 'Surely the darkness shall cover me, and the light about me be night,' even the darkness is not dark to you; the night is bright as the day, for darkness is as light with you."[6]

Arzesh realized that even when she was most ashamed of her life and felt completely alone and utterly bereft, God had been with her. He had never turned His face from her in disgust nor punished her in His rage. The evil that had befallen her was not His doing.

I don't know what it was about these truths that so ministered to my friend's heart, but I could see that they did, and that stirred a deep gratefulness within me. Still, I knew Arzesh carried a profound sadness at the thought of another child growing quietly in her womb.

I drew her attention to the next passage in the psalm. "For you formed my inward parts; you knitted me together in my mother's womb."[7] I looked at Arzesh and a soft picture floated into view. I could see strong hands cradling a tiny, half-formed child. "Right now. Today. In this moment, God is creating your child inside your womb."

Arzesh's eyes widened at the thought. She placed her

hands over her abdomen and peered into the darkness. In that moment, we both recognized the holiness of Arzesh's body. Hidden deep inside her womb, the great God of the universe was quietly, gently knitting together a tiny child.

When we returned to the next sections of the psalm, we read them in the context of this forming child. We talked about God's presence, His hands as it were, cradling such a tender and vulnerable human being who had not yet drawn a single breath. We talked about God's eyes, so full of love, gazing into a person who could not yet form a thought, let alone respond with obedience. We talked about the days of the child's life, days God already knew completely.

Neither Arzesh nor I knew if her child was a son or daughter, strong or lame, smart or stubborn. We could not begin to guess at the child's personality, the obstacles the child would face, nor the traps the child would fall into. We had no way of knowing if the child's life would be an easy one full of generosity, hope, and love, or bitter, full of anger, rage, and hatred. Yet we knew that the great God of the universe was with that child right inside Arzesh's womb. Right there, in the hiddenness of my friend's body, God was loving a child.

Later, when I walked through the narrow streets of Arzesh's refugee community, it occurred to me that there were other things, too, that we didn't know. Perhaps the child would grow up to be a man who would pick up a Kalashnikov or strap on a suicide bomb. Perhaps the child would become a young woman beaten in her husband's home.

The reality that struck me as I stepped over a muddy culvert, fetid with human waste, was quite simple. God loved Arzesh's child wholly and completely, regardless of who that child would become.

The depth and beauty of my conversation with Arzesh has stayed with me and changed the way I see people.

When the gray-bearded one-time-mujahedin taxi driver with his shame and guilt was an unformed child in the darkness of his mother's womb, God had already seen him and loved him. When he cried out with hunger, God fed him.[8] When he stumbled across the floor in his father's home, God taught him to walk.[9]

God saw him and knew him and longed for him even when the chords of human kindness snapped into war, violence, and oppression. Even when he himself did whatever horrible thing it was that covered his face in sadness and collapsed his shoulders in shame.

Just as God loved disobedient, arrogant, sinful Israel, God loves that gray-bearded former mujahedin soldier with an everlasting love birthed from God's own faithfulness.[10] God loves the boy and the gray-bearded man he's become and still has great desires for him. God desires to show him grace and mercy.[11]

God doesn't want to destroy that man, no matter what evil he's done.[12] Instead, God sees the man's bondage and longs to free him.[13] God sees his sin and longs to deliver him.[14] God sees his shame and desires to restore him to honor.[15]

God loves that gray-bearded taxi driver with the haunted

memories just as much as He loves Arzesh's child and the young woman taken by the warlord and raped by his soldiers. Stunningly, God so loves the gray-bearded man, the forming child, and the violated woman that He sent His only begotten Son to save their lives.[16]

And here I must pause because the breadth, length, height, and depth of God's love is so astonishing.

God loves the boys who trip down the street with their white skullcaps and cloth-covered Qurans. God loves the old turbaned men perched on the tops of donkey carts. He loves the burqa-covered women floating like silent clouds down the street. He loves them all.

And this is the thing I must remember, always; the world is full of frightened and frightening men and women whom God loves with a love so rich and so deep that no matter what they do, He still wants to bring them home.

One day, Taliban warriors may step out of their caves into the glorious light of God's love, lay down their Kalashnikovs, and inhale the only peace that can satisfy their souls.[17] "They shall beat their swords into plowshares, and their spears into pruning hooks."[18] And no one will practice war anymore.[19]

One day, the blind and broken, the lame and bereft will find healing and restoration.[20] In that day, "the wolf shall dwell with the lamb, and the leopard shall lie down with the young goat, and the calf and the lion and the fattened calf together; and a little child shall lead them."[21]

This is God's desire, God's plan, the outworking of His eternal and faithful love.

Why does God call us to dangerous places? Because He loves people who live in dangerous places. In fact, He loves people so much that He Himself came to a dangerous place.

DISCUSSION GUIDE

Chapter 3: How Deep the Father's Love

1. Look up Psalm 139:13. How does the truth that God knew and loved you long before you could worship or obey Him impact your heart?

2. Read Psalm 103:2–4. What are your favorite verses that describe God's love for you?

3. Consider Psalm 107:10–14. How do you understand God's love for those who do evil and those who suffer evil?

4. Write out Revelation 22:1–2. How do you imagine heaven?

Chapter 4

GOD CAME FIRST

"Jesus never calls us into a place where He hasn't gone first."

When I think of God coming to a dangerous place, I think first of the Christmas story. It captivates me in its beauty and simplicity.

We see a young woman, pregnant, traveling a hard road. We see a man knocking on doors, finding no room for his wife to rest. We hear of a child born in a place where animals feed.

If we pause here, we might notice the smallness, the ordinariness of the story. A woman delivers a tiny, naked child into the world. She hears His first cry and recognizes one of the most beautiful sounds in all creation. She wraps her baby tightly in a piece of cloth and holds Him next to her heart. She sleeps, grateful, enthralled by her child's warm breath and the soft, rhythmic thumping of His heart against her chest.

It's a lovely story.

If we were Afghans, we would lift our hands to God and

thank Him for a child born alive and healthy. We would breathe a sigh of relief for a mother who survived the ordeal. We might bring the family fruit and perhaps a blanket.

If we were Americans, we would ask after the baby's weight and length. We might send over a brightly wrapped package of onesies and a blue terrycloth snap-up sleep outfit. We would look at pictures and smile at yet another perfectly formed newborn.

The captivating thing about this story is that it's so simple, so normal, and yet it's also astonishing. The God of the universe entered the world as a tiny, helpless newborn, dependent on a young woman for His sustenance and a man for His protection.

The very contradiction is a revolution.

But let's not move on too quickly.

Jesus entered the first-century world as an infant. There were no hospitals, no antiseptics, no antibiotics, and no vitamins. Undoubtedly, Jesus, this God made flesh, was born as a baby into a world where babies often died before their first birthdays. Many others would have died before their fifth.

Young Mary knew this. Her husband did as well.

I pause here to remember that the dangers in the world Jesus entered included cold, heat, malnutrition, and sickness. So many of my friends have carried their own newborn children into places rife with disease, unclean water, and limited medical care.

I pause also to notice young Mary, the mother of this tiny God-with-us child. How normal she is. How human. A new mother holding her firstborn in her arms. I see in her every mother who has nursed an infant, kissed the crown of her child's head, and wondered what joy and pain the future held.

Mary also received a call: to carry the Christ child into the world, to be His mother. There's no way she could fully know the path that lay before her when she said yes to the angel-messenger. Yet she walked that path.

She carried and bore the Christ child. She nursed Him at her breasts, cleaned His messes, pulled Him away from open fires, and held Him when He wept. She loved her child and did everything she could to nurture Him. Certainly she, a mother, knew the world was a very dangerous place.

Then there's Joseph, if not a father by blood, then by action. He saw the dangers crashing around his newborn son. We see him, awakened from a terrifying dream, gathering his small family and leading them to refuge in a foreign land. He, too, did everything he could to protect the helpless infant in his care.

JESUS, THE GREAT GOD of the universe, crossed a distance far greater than the one I had traveled and entered a vulnerability far deeper than the one I experienced. Yet there was, in my own journey, a faint echo of Christ in His.

Now we turn to the infant; seven pounds maybe, unable to roll over, lift His head, or feed Himself. A paradox: the all-powerful Creator and Sustainer of the universe is a small, vulnerable, utterly dependent human being in a very dangerous world.

Jesus never calls us into a place where He hasn't gone first.

⌒

When I left the relative safety and security of my affluent American life, I found myself small, vulnerable, and dependent on strangers in a strange place. I didn't know how to communicate, how to provide for myself, or even how to wear the clothes of the world I entered. I was no longer strong, capable, or independent.

Early in my Afghan journey, circumstances forced me to find a new house to live in. If I'd been in America, the process would've been exhausting but I would have controlled the steps. I would've checked the Internet and local papers for listings. I would've made appointments, jumped in my car, investigated possibilities, and negotiated contracts.

In Afghanistan, I couldn't do any of these things. Instead, I found myself dependent on Afghan friends and neighbors. The first help came in the form of a woman friend. I told her over cups of tea and trays of treats that I needed a new house. A few days later she sent a message to me, carried by a boy: "I found your house."

I asked an Afghan man to be my negotiator and sat by silently as he spoke with the gray-bearded owner. In the end, I accepted the arrangement he made, signed a contract I couldn't read, and moved into the property.

The whole experience and many others like it showed me how deeply dependent I had become.

Jesus, the great God of the universe, crossed a distance far greater than the one I had traveled and entered a vulnerability far deeper than the one I experienced. Yet there was, in my own journey, a faint echo of Christ in His.

Over the years, in very natural ways, Jesus the baby grew into Jesus the man. He walked the dusty roads of Judea and Galilee. He knew hunger and weariness, joy and grief. He felt the pressures of the life He was living. Sometimes He met them and sometimes He withdrew to a quiet place to pray. He slept, ate, undoubtedly smiled, and certainly wept.

And all the while, He encountered people, some who loved Him, some who hated Him. Many misunderstood Him. Some tried to redefine Him while others sought to trap Him. Only in the desert did He walk alone.

Again, I'm reminded of James and John, two young men, minding their own business, working beside their father. Along came Jesus and "He called them,"[1] another very simple thing. "Immediately they left the boat and their father and followed him."[2] They had no idea where the journey would lead them, but they knew that Jesus was the leader and they, His followers.

As their journey unfolded, Jesus helped them understand what following Him meant. First He told them, "Take my yoke upon you, and learn from me."[3] Later He told them, "If anyone would come after me, let him deny himself and take up his cross and follow me."[4]

Follow Me.

See My example and follow Me. I let go of My glory and

came down to this place. Follow Me. I became small and vulnerable. Follow Me. I gave My time, strength, gifts, and abilities in service to those who accepted Me and those who rejected Me. Follow Me.

One day, Jesus sent seventy-two of His followers "into every town and place where he himself was about to go."[5]

I imagine James and John, the young men Jesus called the Sons of Thunder, full of excitement and anticipation, and I recall my own excitement when I sat in the backseat of an old Russian jeep and bounced over donkey trails on my first trip to Afghanistan. The setting sun burned brilliant orange over the brown horizon and I thought *glory!* We drove through walled villages and I watched women covered in blue burqas disappear through wooden gates. I ached to follow them, to sit in their homes, drink tea, and share stories.

I had no idea where my Afghan journey would actually take me. I don't think James and John knew where their journey with Jesus would take them, either. Still, I smile at their nickname, "the Sons of Thunder." How full of themselves they must've been! How so like all of us, like me, like so many others who've climbed onto airplanes to follow Jesus into dangerous places.

I wonder what they thought when Jesus gave them the dramatic warning, "I am sending you out as lambs in the midst of wolves."[6] Perhaps they thought they were strong enough, smart enough, or at the very least, ambassadors of One who was far more powerful than anyone could imagine.

In retrospect, I think they should have heard the echo.

"Behold, the Lamb of God."[7] They should have recognized the invitation to not only serve Jesus, but also to be like Jesus, a lamb, vulnerable, weak, ready for sacrifice even as they walked from village to village. But we don't live in retrospect. We live in the moments to which we've come, and we learn and grow along the way.

James, John, and the others traveled from village to village and "returned with joy, saying, 'Lord, even the demons are subject to us in your name!'"[8]

I can only imagine their celebration. Once again, I see in their joy my own experience.

One afternoon in Afghanistan, over cups of tea and chaotic conversation, Fatima,[9] a woman who had welcomed me into her house, fell into a bitter complaint about the constant pain in her knee and hip.

I only understood about a third of her words, but I definitely recognized the frustration and anger in her face. I also realized that she didn't expect me to do anything about her deteriorating joints. When she completed her diatribe and poured me another cup of tea, I decided to stumble my way through a story.

That was the first time I tried to tell the story of the sick woman who reached out for the hem of Jesus' robe.[10] I didn't do it well, but Fatima was gracious and helped me find the words I was missing. I think by the time I finished, she had forgotten her complaints about her knee and hip. I hadn't. The next part I could say easily, "Fatima Jan. The Honorable Jesus Messiah is healer."

My friend nodded. "Yes, yes. He's a prophet."

"He said if we are sick, we can pray. Can I pray for you?"

Fatima nodded again. "Yes. Yes. Thank you. Praise be to God!"

I realized immediately that she did not expect me to pray at that very moment, but that was certainly my intention. "Now? Fatima Jan?"

She was shocked. *You want to pray now? Here? For me?* It didn't take her long to say yes.

That presented me with another problem. I couldn't for the life of me remember how to say hip or knee. I decided that I could stumble through my prayer just as I had stumbled through the story of the sick woman, and so I did. The prayer didn't take very long. It went something like this. "All-powerful Creator of the universe, Healer Jesus Messiah, please heal Fatima Jan's . . . what's this called? . . . knee . . . and . . . what's this called? . . . hip. Amen."

As soon as I finished praying, Fatima urged me to drink more tea. She seemed pleased that I had prayed, but said no more about it.

A couple of weeks later, I found myself again in Fatima's house. This time, a group of neighborhood women joined us for tea and treats. One old woman complained bitterly of pain in her hips. At that, Fatima leaned forward and said quite simply, "You should ask the foreigner to pray for you. She prayed for my knee and my hip, and they have become healed."

I was delighted. In fact, I was more than delighted. I could barely contain my joy. Look, Jesus healed my friend. I prayed and Jesus healed my friend. How cool is that? I'm sure I wrote something just like that in my subsequent email home.

I can barely imagine how delighted the seventy-two were when they returned to Jesus so full of wonderful stories! How excited they must have been! But Jesus didn't encourage such a focus on outcomes. Instead, He warned His followers against it. "Do not rejoice in this, that the spirits are subject to you, but rejoice that your names are written in heaven."[11]

Here, I take both warning and deep encouragement.

When things were going well and their work was fruitful, James and John could certainly rejoice in the astonishing outcomes they witnessed: the deaf heard, the blind saw, the lame leapt with joy.

But Jesus knew there were other outcomes ahead; they would soon face suffering and loss deeper than James, John, or the other seventy could imagine. He invited them to focus not on the outcomes but, ironically, on themselves. "Rejoice that your names are written in heaven."

Immediately, I want to protest. "But it's not about me. It's about You and serving You out in the world. Isn't it?"

I wonder if James and John remembered this teaching when they sat in the upper room and watched Jesus break a piece of bread. I wonder if they thought about it when the soldiers came to the garden and carried away their beloved teacher. I wonder if they held on to it through the long hours of Jesus' passion.

Circumstances change. We have times when the journey

is glorious, when we're full of joy and excitement. Other times the darkness closes in on us and all we see is failure, loss, and destruction.

Certainly, Jesus knew this. He knew it for Himself and His own journey, and He knew it for us in the paths we would walk. "In the world you will have tribulation."[12] "Beware of men, for they will deliver you over to courts and flog you in their synagogues, and you will be dragged before governors and kings."[13] "You will be hated by all nations for my name's sake."[14]

What a contradiction to the excitement of village-to-village ministry, feeding thousands, and watching their teacher heal the sick of every conceivable disease!

I imagine James, John, and the others struggling to understand. I'm sure that in those days, with Jesus alive in a human body, the warnings He offered could only be dark and incomprehensible. Yet they had heard those warnings, just as we, before we boarded airplanes to dangerous places, understood that we were walking into a darkness so deep it might someday overwhelm us.

We counted the cost, at least as well as we could. We each said, "He's worth it. Jesus is worth it."

It's John who recounts the story that draws my attention here. He and the others were working with Jesus at a safe distance from Jerusalem. They knew that Jerusalem was a desperately dangerous place. They'd heard more than enough reports of the men in the city who wanted to kill their beloved teacher.[15] Plus, Jesus Himself had told them that the elders, chief priests, and scribes would hurt and kill Him.[16]

They also knew that a friend in Judea was desperately ill.[17] Still, they couldn't imagine going, at least not until Jesus said, "Let us go to Judea again."[18]

John tells us the disciples hesitated. Of course they did. They understood the dangers far too clearly to simply follow blindly. And blind following was not what Jesus requested, anyway—He wanted their eyes on Him, not the danger. By that point in the story, He'd been quite open about what lay ahead.

The followers of Jesus faced a Rubicon, a decision point that would irrevocably change their lives. In that moment, knowing the dangers that awaited them, they chose to follow Jesus. It was Thomas who articulated the decision. "Let us also go, that we may die with him."[19]

Here is another place where we should pause.

We see James, John, Thomas, and the other disciples agreeing to go to Jerusalem, but they did not lead themselves. They followed Jesus all the way into the very dangerous city of Jerusalem.

As the days unfolded, they watched Jesus pick up the bread and break it. They listened as He spoke of a covenant made with His blood. They stood back as He

JESUS DIDN'T SEND James, John, Thomas, or Mary to a place He hadn't gone to first.

was arrested. They hid as He was carried away. They heard the jeering crowd, the strike of the hammer against the nails, and the pain-wracked groan of the One they loved. They sat in dark silence, weak with despair, through the long weekend.

James, John, Thomas, Mary, and the others saw the bitter triumph of evil over all they counted as good and beautiful. But it was Jesus who endured the suffering.

Jesus turned His face to Jerusalem. Jesus recognized the danger closing in on Him.[20] He gave His hands to be bound. Jesus was mocked and tortured, and He felt the weight of His own cross and the searing pain of the nails driven through His hands and feet. He knew the separation from God and angelic protection, felt the weight of our sins. Jesus lay, dead, in the grave.

Jesus didn't send James, John, Thomas, or Mary to a place He hadn't gone to first.

After the cross, after the resurrection, after the ascension, James, John, and the others carried their faith and the Spirit Christ had given them into a brutally dangerous world. If they hadn't, not one of us would be reading His book, opening our hearts in prayer, or sharing in the bread and cup that marks the death and resurrection of our Lord and Savior.

The horrific stories of their sufferings, and the sufferings of so many others, have come down to us through the centuries. Of course, the stories disturb us. They should. Christ came to give us life, abundant life.[21] That's His eternal desire for us. But the enemy is still alive, still robbing, killing, and destroying.[22] The world is a dangerous place. And yet Jesus says; "I have overcome the world."[23]

When we go into the world with Christ,[24] we go as lambs among wolves.[25] Yes, we are small and vulnerable, just as Jesus entered the world small and vulnerable. We follow Him in every way we can, knowing that He never leads us where He Himself has not gone first. We carry in our very human hands and hearts an invitation—God's invitation to each member of the human community.

DISCUSSION GUIDE

Chapter 4: God Came First

1. Consider the Christmas story. What do you think when you consider God coming into this world as a small and vulnerable baby?

2. Has God ever led you into a situation where you felt vulnerable? What was that like for you?

3. Have you ever experienced God's peace in a difficult situation? How did your experience of peace affect you?

4. Consider Matthew 26:36–46. What do you notice about Jesus' prayer and ultimate decision?

5. Where is God calling you in this season of your life? Journal a prayer of surrender.

Chapter 5

GOD WANTS TO FILL HIS TABLE

"We go because God wants to bring all His precious, beautiful, wounded, frightened, lost children home."

Often, when I hadn't visited an Afghan family in a week or two, they would welcome me back into their home with a gentle chiding. "Where have you been? Your place has become empty."

I love that expression, "Your place has become empty." It makes me feel safe, welcome. Oh, I have a place and because I've been absent, that place has been empty.

I knew they weren't talking about a physical location like a chair at the table. For one thing, they didn't use chairs or tables. We sat on cotton floor mats in rooms that also served as dining rooms and bedrooms.

No, they meant something entirely different. They meant that they had missed my voice, my smile and laughter, my presence.

They also meant that I belonged with them, in their conversation, their community.

"Your place has become empty and therefore, we've missed you."

Now that I'm back in America, I'm well aware of the empty spaces occupied by my Afghan friends. They are no longer flesh-and-blood participants in my life. Instead, they have become like unsubstantial holograms present only in memory.

We all know this experience. Each of us has people we've come to love and now can't quite reach. We feel the emptiness of their absence and long for their presence.

The other reason I love this expression is that it opened another door for me to understand the heart of God. I imagine Jesus saying to Aziza and Ahmad and Suliman and Shukria, "Your place is empty. Come. Come."

<hr />

Once again, I think of John, the follower of Jesus, only now he's much older. His heart has been broken, healed, and broken again. His brother is dead and he's been exiled to a harsh, desolate island. There, he prays and receives the most astonishing vision.

Tucked in the middle of his account, John writes, "Then I heard what seemed to be the voice of a great multitude, like the roar of many waters and like the sound of mighty peals of thunder, crying out, 'Hallelujah! For the Lord our God the Almighty reigns.'"[1]

I've always been captivated by the scene John describes.

I envision "a great multitude that no one could number, from every nation, from all tribes and peoples and languages."[2] I see wheat-colored Afghans, coffee-colored Africans, cinnamon-colored Indians, mustard-colored Asians, and ginger-colored Europeans—a kaleidoscope of beautiful earth tones. I imagine languages: Czech, Bengali, Urdu, Dutch, English, Swahili, and every other tongue ever used by people throughout the history of the world, all interwoven into one holy, comprehensible expression of perfect worship.

I imagine faces: my grandparents, my parents and siblings, my American and European friends, my Afghan friends, and a billion others, all bathed in glorious light.

And suddenly, almost inexplicably, John writes, "Blessed are those who are invited to the marriage supper of the Lamb."[3]

A party.

In the middle of the heavenly scene, there is a party, a grand celebration.

I can't help but picture this scene through Afghan lenses. The family has stretched a green, gold, and brown canopy across the open space of their walled compound. They've covered the ground with borrowed carpets. They've purchased several sheep, huge bags of rice, and smaller bags of raisins and julienne carrots. They've borrowed glass plates, cups, and tea thermoses from every neighbor.

They've sent out their invitations, handwritten cards with flowers printed on the front, delivered by the hands of small children who've run through dusty streets and knocked on wooden gates. If I've received an invitation, I must go. I might have a day's notice, if I'm lucky. But never mind, I can't go to work. I have a wedding to attend! And everyone understands.

By the time we arrive, the sheep have been slaughtered and the meat is cooking. Men stand around kettle drum–sized pots of steaming spiced rice laced with carrots and raisins. The musicians begin to play.

In indoor rooms or beneath the outdoor canopy, women guests gather barefooted, but dressed in our finest clothes. We clasp hands and trade kisses and greetings. We take our places on carpets, hip to hip between our neighbors. We talk and laugh and catch up on one another's news.

More women arrive and greetings are exchanged. We laugh with delight at the presence of friends we've not seen in months and strangers we've never met, but now count as family. We are intoxicated with the joy of community, the energy of a colorful, ebullient celebration.

The steaming rice topped with thick blocks of meat is served on oval platters, one plate for two people. We dip our fingers into the rice and make sure our partner has an equal or better share of the meat.

When the meal is finished, we laugh and take our turns dancing in the open space between folded knees and clapping hands. We pull our shoulders back, tilt our heads, and shape our dance with the fine movements of wrists and fingers. We celebrate with all we are and all we have, and in that moment, nothing outside the walls of our celebration exists.

When it's time, reluctantly we bid our goodbyes, slip into our shoes, and return to the brown, dusty Afghan world.

A friend in America once asked me what Afghan women do for diversion, for fun. It took me a while to figure it out but then I remembered. "We go to weddings."

And if I received an invitation, hand delivered to my gate by a boy or a little girl, and didn't put on my sparkly outfit and share in the plates of rice and joyous dancing, then my Afghan friends would chide me. "Where were you? Your place became empty."

I recall a story Jesus shared when He walked the dusty streets of first-century Judea. "The kingdom of heaven may be compared to a king who gave a wedding feast for his son, and sent his servants to call those who were invited to the wedding feast, but they would not come. Again he sent other servants, saying, 'Tell those who are invited, "See, I have prepared my dinner, my oxen and my fat calves have been slaughtered, and everything is ready. Come to the wedding feast."'"[4]

I imagine the king, the father of the groom, preparing his home to receive the guests who would celebrate his most joyous day. "My son is marrying. Come. Come and celebrate."

He's planned and prepared everything. The canopy has been spread. The carpets are stretched out on the ground. The musicians have tuned their instruments. The host has spared no expense, withheld no blessing. All is ready.

I imagine his shock, his disappointment and anger, when he discovers that those whom he invited will not come.[5] He's prepared his celebration and wants his home full of guests. There are too many empty places and so he sends out more invitations. "Go out quickly to the streets and lanes of the city, and bring in the poor and crippled and blind and lame."[6]

His servants run through the dusty streets. This time, they don't knock on gates but instead find the beggars sitting beside the road. They press invitations into their hands and bid them come. And they do. The poor, the crippled, the blind, and the lame of the city come to the king's wedding.

But the king's house is big and still there is room. He longs for his house to be full, so once again he sends out more invitations. "Go out to the highways and hedges and compel people to come in, that my house may be filled."[7]

His servants leave the safety and security of the lanes and streets of the city. They search the highways and along the hedges for whoever they can find: strangers, foreigners, men and women of different tribes, nations, and tongues. They compel them to come in. "Come. My master has prepared a feast. Come."

I cannot help but think that Jesus' parable describes exactly the heart of Father God, a Father who even now is preparing a wedding feast for His Son. Already, He sees the guests: celebrants from every tribe, nation, and tongue; Uzbeks and Pashtuns, Scots and Poles, Libyan Sawknah, Sudanese Rufaiyin, Indian Kotwali, and Han Chinese. People whose skin spans the colors of the ground from which we were made, all clothed in clean white linen, all gathered at the feast God's been preparing since the foundation of the world.

I imagine Father God, delighted that finally the long-awaited celebration has come; the guests are eating and dancing, rejoicing in the glory of His home. I imagine His deep satisfaction, His joy and His delight.

But that day hasn't come yet. Jesus is still preparing a place[8] and we're still delivering invitations.

Why does God call us to dangerous places, to the highways and the hedges of the world? Because God's house is not yet full. Because there are places that are empty and guests who have not yet received their invitation.

How big is God's house? I don't know, but big enough that He desires that none should perish but that all should turn and come.[9]

So we, God's servants, go, our Master's invitation in our hands, out to the highways and hedges. We walk through squalid refugee camps in Syria, fetid open-air trash dumps in Mozambique, drug-infested smoky brothels in Bangkok. We go because deep in the Pamir Mountains of Tajikistan and out on the dusty plains of Iraq, there are people whom God wants to come to His feast. There are people hidden away in small villages in Kyrgyzstan and

THE FEAST GOD INVITES us to is greater than any we've ever experienced. The wedding at Cana when Jesus turned water into wine is but a shadow compared to the glory that awaits us. Every joyful celebration we've ever experienced in this life is like a black-and-white sketch that helps us dream the magnificence of what lies ahead.

Kazakhstan who belong at God's table. There are women in Somalia; street kids in Portland, Oregon; girls in northern Nigeria;
and men in Chechnya and a thousand other places who belong
in God's house.

God sees them, every one of them, people drawing water
from open wells, drinking tea in mud houses, scheming evil in
dark camps, hiding from violence in rough caves. He knows
their names and faces and voices and laughter and tears. He
knows their fears and dreams and joys and sorrows.

He was there when they were born, when they fell down,
and when they got up—and He wants to share the blessings
of all He has with them. This is the heart of God—generous,
loving, kind, patient—always ready to bless.

He's prepared His table from the foundations of the earth,
and there is still room.

Some, like those initially invited in Jesus' parable,[10] will receive their invitation and reject it. Others will refuse the invitation and mistreat the messengers who deliver it.[11] Still others
will disrespect the invitation and the God who invites them.[12]

Yet, in heaven, there will be a party and the guests will come
"from every nation, from all tribes and peoples and languages."[13]
They'll be clothed in "fine linen, bright and pure,"[14] and the
sound of their celebration will be glorious![15]

I can scarcely imagine the wholeness of our joy. We will
see God face-to-face and live in the unfiltered light of His presence.[16] We'll worship Him with complete and unashamed aban-

don.[17] Our wounds will be healed[18] and every tear we've ever shed will be wiped away.[19]

The feast God invites us to is greater than any we've ever experienced. The wedding at Cana[20] when Jesus turned water into wine is but a shadow compared to the glory that awaits us. Every joyful celebration we've ever experienced in this life is like a black-and-white sketch that helps us dream the magnificence of what lies ahead.

And so once again I return to the experience of an Afghan wedding. I recall one gathering in the home of a poor friend. My friend's house was small, but every room was packed with guests. We had each traveled down mud-soaked roads and had arrived damp and cold, but the warmth of so many celebrants helped us forget the grayness beyond the walls.

Inside the unpainted room where I sat between brightly clothed guests, the tablecloth was spread on the floor and covered with the most humble treats: raisins, almonds, chickpeas, cakes and cookies purchased from a local bakery, and cups of tea. This was the celebration of a poor family, and I was honored to be there.

When I first arrived, I didn't know most of the guests in the small room I chose. Still we laughed, teased one another, and traded stories. With tea and conversation, we became friends, and that was a beautiful gift.

Later, when the dancing began, guests moved from room to room. That's when I discovered a surprise. In each room I entered, the delighted greetings of Afghan and foreign friends welcomed me. "You're here! I'm so happy! How do you know this family?" With clasped hands we kissed one another's cheeks and traded connections.

"I am a friend of the bride's cousin."

"I work with the groom's brother."

"I've known the mother of the bride for years."

"We were neighbors during the war."

"We grew up in the same village."

We traced the threads of one another's relationships, delighted in our shared community.

That humble celebration is one of the most joyous I can recall from all my years in Afghanistan. It was like a family reunion, but unexpected, with a fresh surprise through each doorway.

Once again, an experience in this world helps me to dream of heaven. Who will I see? My grandmother welcoming me into an embrace I've missed for years? Friends, family members, people I barely knew, and others who've been dear to me all my life? I ache for the rejoicing of seeing again those whose losses I've grieved.

I can only imagine what we'll be like. The apostle Paul tells us that we will be transformed; our natural bodies will die, and our spiritual bodies will rise alive.[21] Somehow, we'll be like Jesus after He emerged from death,[22] different, yet recognizable.[23]

Will we look around God's heavenly table and see those we've loved here on earth? I think we will. Just as the apostle Paul expected to see his beloved Thessalonians,[24] I expect to see my beloved Afghans: Asina,[25] whose hand I held when the cancer consumed her body; Amina, who prayed with me when the rain soaked the mud and we knew we'd never see each other in Afghanistan again; Khalid, who hid his printed pages of the book of Ephesians in his jacket pocket; Nik Mohammed, who rubbed his beard and shared his stories of traveling the harsh road back from Iran; and many, many others.

I imagine we'll look around the table with joy-filled delight. "You made it." "You're here." "I'm so glad to see you."

Perhaps we'll see for the first time the intricate tapestry of our shared lives, not only our conversations with one another, but our prayers and gifts as well. Perhaps my American friends will look into the faces of Afghans for whom they've prayed yet never met and rejoice to see them at the table. "Ah, you are Asina! I'm so glad to finally meet you."

Can you imagine what a day of rejoicing that will be?

I'm reminded of the story of an Afghan friend. Josef[26] was captured by the Taliban during the worst days of the war. They beat him with cables and then transported him across the country and locked him into a dank, overcrowded prison. For nine months he languished, terrified, abandoned. After six months, the International Red Cross visited his prison and gave him a blanket. That's all, just a blanket, but that blanket meant everything to him.

When Josef told me the story of the blanket, tears filled his eyes. "In nine months, only one good thing happened to me. The foreigners gave me a blanket." At that, he looked past me, his eyes lost in the memory. When he returned, he said something very simple, something beautiful. "I knew God had not forgotten me."

Perhaps one day Josef will see the person who gave the check that paid for the blanket and the men who delivered it to him in that dark prison. Can you imagine?

I want to be at that table. I want to see the faces and hear the stories of each and every once blind, lame, crippled person whose journey has brought them to the greatest celebration we can ever know. I want to rejoice in the sheer glory of God's grace poured out in blessings upon blessings.

And as much as I long to be there, I know that God's heart is full of a greater desire than I can even imagine. Only God understands the extreme loss of human fellowship that we experienced with Him and with one another in the garden.[27] Only God knows the riches He longs to share with us. Only God knows what could be.

Once again, I look to human experience to help me imagine. I see a mother glowing in her son's wedding, celebrating the beauty and grace of her daughter-in-law. I see a grandmother sitting at her Thanksgiving table, surrounded by her children and grandchildren, delighted that all of her family has come home and her table is full.

These are shadows of God's heart, echoes of His love.

Jesus showed us the Father's aching desire when He stood over Jerusalem and wept. "How often would I have gathered your children together as a hen gathers her brood under her wings, and you were not willing!"[28] He shows us the Father's search for the separated one in the parable of the lost sheep.[29] He shows us the Father's joy in the story of the prodigal son, when the father lifts his eyes, sees his child, and runs to him.[30] God runs to us.

This is the heart of God, a desire so deep, so rich, so strong that He spares nothing to bring His children home.

Why do we go out to the highways and hedges, to war-torn countries and disease-ridden communities? We go because God wants to bring all His precious, beautiful, wounded, frightened, lost children home.

Still, we ask, isn't there another way? Do we have to hand-deliver God's invitations?

DISCUSSION GUIDE

Chapter 5: God Wants to Fill His Table

1. Consider Revelation 19:6. Who would you like to see in heaven with you? Pray for them by name right now.

2. Read Matthew 22:1–10. How would you describe the guests at the banquet?

3. How would you describe the King in Jesus' Matthew 22:1–10 parable?

4. Read 2 Peter 3:9. Write out the verse and read it aloud. What is our Father's heart and desire like?

5. In Luke 15:3–7, Jesus tells the parable of the shepherd seeking a single lost sheep. Think about the lost sheep. What might it be experiencing while the shepherd is looking for it?

6. Journal about how He found you when you were wandering as a lost sheep. Write a prayer of praise for His rescue of you.

Chapter 6

THEY HAVE TO
HEAR, SEE, TOUCH

*"But how can they call on him to save them unless they believe in him?
And how can they believe in him if they have never heard about him?
And how can they hear about him unless someone tells them?"*
—Romans 10:14 NLT

The first time I went to Afghanistan, a woman covered in a light blue burqa grabbed my hand and through her tears and the help of a translator told me of the day she lost seven sons in one Taliban bomb.

As I stood in front of her, I had no idea what to say or do. There was no way I could return her sons to her. No way that I could heal her emotional, physical, or economic losses. In that moment, I wondered what she wanted from me, what she thought I could give her.

She was squatting on the dusty ground with a group of

other burqa-clad women in a food distribution line. She carried a smudged scrap of paper in her hand that entitled her to a bag of flour. Did she expect something more from me?

I struggled with how to respond. I looked into the eyes of my translator and found no help. I turned my heart toward God and in desperation prayed, "Lord, what do I say?"

When I looked back at the woman, I saw her tears streaming over her cheeks. I knelt on the ground and, with my own tears, shared her loss. I knew, even as I did, that Christ shared her loss as well, that when He suffered the brutal horror of His passion, He loved this treasured, grieving mother. I knew He saw her pain and that He was with us in the intense sorrow we were experiencing.

Through my translator, I told the mother that I was sad, deeply sad for her loss. She nodded her head and together we wept. After a few moments, I told her that God sees her and that He loves her. She closed her eyes and laid her forehead against our clasped hands. When she lifted her face and looked into my eyes, she nodded again. The pain in her face had softened.

WHY DOES GOD CALL us to dangerous places? Because He desires to show His love to people who live in dangerous places.

She laid her calloused hand on my cheek and whispered a word of praise. "*Shukr-e-khuda,*" thanks be to God.

In that brief conversation, that holy exchange, a bereft mother experienced a moment of comfort and inhaled an eternal truth: God sees her, loves her, and shares in her suffering.

The God of the universe had taken on flesh and touched a woman. That day, the flesh was mine. Within me, I carried the presence of Christ.[1]

This is a mystery we recognize and acknowledge but struggle to articulate. After all, we are just human, an American woman and an Afghan woman holding hands and crying in a dusty Afghan courtyard.

Why does God call us to dangerous places? Because He desires to show His love to people who live in dangerous places.

As I let go of the woman's hand and stepped away, I knew that I had offered far more love and truth than could possibly be given from 7,400 miles away. I knew that she would never forget that brief exchange, that moment of not only meeting a blue-eyed foreigner, but more importantly, of experiencing comfort and love.

I'm reminded of the beautiful words of Saint Teresa of Avila.

Christ has no body but yours,
No hands, no feet on earth but yours,
Yours are the eyes with which he looks
Compassion on this world,
Yours are the feet with which he walks to do good,
Yours are the hands with which he blesses
    all the world.[2]

Have you ever kissed the skinned knee of a crying child, held the hand of a woman giving birth, or sat quietly beside a dying parent? If you have, then you know there's something powerful in being present.

I never saw that Afghan mother again and have no idea what became of her. Perhaps she collected her food and returned to her home, grateful for the flour and the kindness of the stranger she'd met. Perhaps she was disappointed that I hadn't given her more. Or, perhaps, she was aware that God had met her and she found comfort and strength in His love.

As for me, I would like to have given her more: money to sustain her in her poverty; justice against those who'd taken her sons; and a fuller story of who God is, how much He loves her, and what He's done on her behalf. But that brief exchange in the presence of so many others limited what I could give.

And here's a place of trust. The kingdom of God is like a mustard seed,[3] so small and irrelevant, planted in a weeping woman's heart. I look to God to grow that seed.

Over the years, I've had the privilege of hearing the stories of many Afghans who've come to follow Christ. Virtually all share the same six common experiences.

- Each has met a Christ-follower, usually a foreigner but sometimes a fellow Afghan.
- Each has heard or read a fragment of Scripture in the form of a story, movie, radio program, or the written text itself.

- Each experienced a dream or a vision in which God revealed Himself to them personally.
- That combination of experiences led each person to count the extreme cost of following Christ in the dangerous lands in which they lived.
- Those who committed their lives to Christ usually did so alone and under cover of darkness.
- Later, they experienced persecution and, if they held on to their faith, returned to tell their story.

For most, the journey required years. For some, a lifetime.

I've taken great comfort and encouragement in hearing those stories and finding my own story in them. My part in Afghanistan was to be the presence of Christ, the Christ-follower many Afghans met in their midst. My part was also to share the truth of who God is with those whom He loves.

God's part is to reveal Himself in mysterious ways we can neither predict nor control. Christianity is, at its most fundamental, a religion of revelation. God revealed Himself to Abraham, Isaac, and Jacob. He revealed Himself to Moses, Samuel, and the prophets and many of the kings of Israel. He revealed Himself at the Jordan River when He declared, "This is my beloved Son, with whom I am well pleased."[4] He revealed Himself after the resurrection to Mary, Peter, James and John, Thomas, the disciples on the Emmaus road, and many others.[5]

And when He did, their lives were transformed.

Once again, my thoughts return to James and John. I imagine the two brothers, hiding behind a locked door,[6] grieving the loss of their beloved teacher. John had already seen the empty tomb and the grave clothes lying on the rock.[7] His friend Peter had seen it as well. Still, "they did not understand the Scripture, that he [Jesus] must rise from the dead."[8]

If the story stopped there, we wouldn't have a New Testament and none of us would know God in Christ. John and James would likely have returned to their father and taken up their lives as fishermen. The teacher Jesus would have become a memory whose stories they shared while mending nets, but nothing more.

Fortunately for us, the story doesn't end there. The Scriptures say that "Jesus came and stood among them."[9] He entered the closed room where His followers hid dejected and revealed Himself to them. He spoke to them. "Peace be with you. As the Father has sent me, even so I am sending you." And when He had said this, He breathed on them and said to them, "Receive the Holy Spirit."[10]

This experience, this revelation, transformed the lives of James, John, and the others. They might fish, but fishing would not be their occupation. They had come to know the risen Christ, and history shows us that they did go, just as Christ sent them.

I don't know if that grieving Afghan mother I met at the flour distribution ever experienced a revelation of Christ that transformed her life. In this, I can only trust God, and I'm grateful for that freedom. It allows me to do my part, to be the Christ-follower that she met and to share some fragment of truth with her.

Why does God send us into dangerous places? That we might be the Christ-followers others meet.

Jesus took on flesh and dwelt among us,[11] Emmanuel, God with us.[12]

When we go to dangerous places, to places where there are few if any Christ-followers, we go as Christ's ambassadors,[13] but we don't go alone. We carry the presence of Christ with us,[14] the hope of glory.[15] We love, serve, heal, and help those who are weary and heavy laden. In doing so, we reveal God's love and compassion to a hurting world.

Yet we don't just reveal God's love; we reveal His truth as well. We offer His invitation, reconciling others to God.[16]

Afghan Christ-followers always speak of having encountered a fragment of Scripture; sometimes in the form of a story, movie, radio program, or the written text itself.

I've had the privilege of listening to Christian radio programs in Afghanistan and have been amazed that Afghans could hear them. I've heard of Afghans watching Christian teaching programs via satellite TV. These stories are rare, but they happen, and I'm grateful for all who make them possible.

Still, most people who live in dangerous places can't access such resources. Instead, they rely on the stories shared by their neighbors and friends or the fragments of Scripture that reach their hands.

Once, while I was visiting the home of an Afghan friend,

I encountered a young woman who seemed uncomfortable in the gathering. She was dressed completely in black while the other women wore colorful headscarves and brightly patterned dresses. She sat silent and stiff, back straight, knees together, shins flat against the floor. The other women sat cross-legged, laughed, told stories, and teased one another.

Through the course of the conversation, I learned that the young woman was a returnee from Iran, a conservative Shiite whose family traced their roots from the prophet Mohammed. As a descendant of the prophet, she held a rank of honor. She was also a university student, educated while the rest of the women were completely illiterate. That, too, gave her status yet also separated her from the other women. As a returnee, she had experienced an entirely different world and still carried its marks. It was no wonder she was uncomfortable in our gathering.

When it was time for me to leave, I rose from the floor, bid my goodbyes, and stepped out into a narrow, mud-brick-walled alley full of playing children. I was surprised to find the young woman behind me. I attempted to walk beside her, but she separated herself from me.

I continued down the alley, greeting the children as I went, uncomfortably aware of the young woman who walked silently a few paces behind me.

When the alleyway turned sharply, the young woman caught up to me. She grabbed the elbow of my long coat with her fingertips and spoke to me in a rushed whisper. I stopped and turned toward her. I had no idea what she'd said.

She looked up and down the alleyway and then asked her question again. "Do you have the book of the Honorable Jesus Messiah?"

I stiffened. There had been nothing in this young woman's demeanor to lead me to believe that she was in the least bit interested in the Honorable Jesus Messiah or in His book. I wondered if I had encountered a trap. After all, she was a conservative Shiite returnee from Iran. I couldn't make sense of her request.

I imagine she saw my hesitance. She tugged at my elbow and demanded that I walk, and so the two of us continued down the alley, but this time side by side. As we walked, she shared her story in the thickly accented Farsi of Iran.

I struggled to follow, but caught her meaning.

She had been born in Afghanistan and carried, as a small child, to Iran. There, she attended school. When she was a teenager, she met a Christ-follower. The two girls became friends, but only for a brief season, until her brothers objected. But before that happened, the Iranian Christ-follower invited her to go to church for a Christmas Eve service. There, she saw something she'd never seen before or since, and she wanted to know what it was. Finally, her story complete, she asked again, "Do you have the book of the Honorable Jesus Messiah?"

I took a deep breath and decided that the young woman's story was genuine and thanked God for the Christ-follower she'd met in Iran. I knew I had my own copy of the New Testament in the Dari language safely wrapped in a clean cloth in my backpack. I explained to the young woman that it was my copy and that she could borrow it. She readily agreed.

We paused, side by side, in the alley. I slipped my hand into my bag, found the book of Jesus wrapped in its clean cloth, and handed it to the young woman.

She took the book, touched it to her forehead, and slid it into her purse. A moment later, she was gone. She'd disappeared around the corner of the alley back toward the house from which we'd come.

I was left standing in the Afghan sun, surrounded by playing children, amazed at what had just happened. Where else, in that dangerous place, could a young returnee from Iran receive a copy of the Scriptures?

I knew she couldn't walk into a bookstore, religious or otherwise, and purchase a New Testament. I doubted if she had access to the Internet and was sure there was no satellite TV in her home.

Yet here I was, a courier, carrying Christ's invitation in my bag.

In America, we have churches in every community, Bibles in every bookstore, and teachings on every TV. We have easy Internet access and with it teachings of every kind.

Afghans don't have any of these things. Most will only encounter a fragment of Scripture if someone carrying Scripture in their stories or their bag walks among them.

And this is another reason God calls us to dangerous places. After all, "How can they believe in him if they have never heard about him? And how can they hear about him unless someone tells them?"[17]

Jesus stood before James, John, and the others in His resurrected glory. His words come down to us through the centuries. "Go."[18] Go and shine My light in the darkness. Go and carry My fragrance[19] to those who are lost. Go and declare what you've seen and heard of Me.[20] Go.

And so we go, carrying Christ's presence in us. We share His love and His truth. Along the way, we meet people. Some welcome us into their homes and their lives. Others push us away.

Like James and John before us, we struggle with rejection. When James and John felt rejection's sting, they wanted to punish those who had so offended them.[21] I understand their reaction.

There was a particular village in Afghanistan where an Afghan woman friend lived. I visited her there a few times. On my third visit, I encountered the afterglow of a wedding party. Relatives had come from all over the country to celebrate the marriage of a family member.

When I arrived in the village, I was ushered into a large room packed with at least forty people, men and women, all sitting on the floor, lining the walls. A bowl of soup and a fragment of bread were placed before me. I felt awkward eating alone, but knew that the guests had already eaten and rejecting the food would have been an offense.

I searched the room for the host and chose the most senior man. I explained that I was a follower of the Honorable Jesus

Messiah and that it was my practice to pray before eating. I asked his permission to do so.

The old man stroked his long beard and blinked his eyes to communicate his assent.

IN THE COURSE OF our conversation, I explained the Trinity, who Jesus is, that He died and why, and what it means to be a Christ-follower. I felt the intense scrutiny of every member of the gathering and knew I wasn't safe. I also knew that Christ calls us to give a defense for the faith that is within us and so I did, as gently, respectfully, and honestly as I could.

With his permission, I lifted my hands and prayed both a blessing on the family and my gratefulness to God for the food. Then I began to eat. All the while, the people stared at me.

It didn't take long for one of the young men to rise from his place next to the wall. He sat down on the floor a few feet in front of me and studied me carefully. I struggled to hide my discomfort.

I glanced at him a few times and took the measure of the man. He was young, perhaps thirty, and clean-shaven. He wore Western clothes: a plaid button-down shirt and a pair of blue jeans.

After what felt like an eternity, the young man broke his silence. He explained that he was a translator for the Dutch military and had come home to celebrate his family's wedding. He thought that he knew what Christianity was from his exposure to the Dutch and questioned me closely. It was clear that he wanted to prove his expertise and his commitment to Islam.

At first, he delivered his questions in English, but I responded in Dari and so he switched over to his mother tongue. As we talked, the rest of the family stared in silence and I struggled to field his questions, remain calm, and finish the meal the family had served me.

In the course of our conversation, I explained the Trinity, who Jesus is, that He died and why, and what it means to be a Christ-follower. I felt the intense scrutiny of every member of the gathering and knew I wasn't safe. I also knew that Christ calls us to give a defense for the faith that is within us and so I did, as gently, respectfully, and honestly as I could.[22]

After I finished the meal and had sat long enough to honor my hosts, I rose from the floor and asked permission to leave. I didn't relax until I was safely back in my Afghan home.

The next day, I received a message delivered by the old bearded man who'd given me permission to pray. He didn't speak to me personally, but rather delivered his message to one of my Afghan staff members. "You must not return to our village."

Later, I learned that the men of that village had spent all evening in their mosque discussing me and the things I'd shared. They'd argued, disagreed, and finally agreed: I could not return.

I wasn't surprised. Jesus said this sort of thing would happen. He said it was part of the journey: "And if anyone will not receive you or listen to your words, shake off the dust from your feet when you leave that house or town."[23]

I understood the anger and frustration James and John

must've experienced when the village didn't welcome Jesus and His followers.[24] They wanted to punish that village, but Jesus would have none of it. Instead, they simply went to another village.[25]

Jesus said to go—and while you're going, build relationships, introduce people to Me, and invite them to follow Me, to become My disciples.

Not everyone who lives in a dangerous place will receive us, but some will.

I had the privilege of meeting with a group of women in a community outside of one of the cities in which I lived. Each week, we gathered, drank tea, listened to Scripture, sang, and prayed. There were usually six of us, plus children. Some of the women were Christ-followers. Others were still considering.

I remember one particular gathering. It was summer and the afternoon sun was hot, but we sat on the floor in a cool basement room. Above us, the young men of the family clustered around the open window. We knew they were there. We knew they were watching us, listening, and that they could decide if we would continue to meet.

That day, one of the young girls read the Scripture passage. She read it five times through before her illiterate grandmothers decided it was enough. We lifted our hands and prayed for guidance and understanding. Then we discussed the passage.

While we talked, the young men listened through the window above us.

When we finished discussing the passage, we prayed for one

another, and when we finished praying, we sang. We lifted our hands, closed our eyes, and sang one of the most beautiful worship songs I've ever known. The English translation of the Dari words are beautiful:

Holy, Holy, Holy, oh God, all powerful God.
Who was, who is, who is to come.
Fill the heavens and earth with Your glory.
Worthy, Worthy, Worthy,
Worthy is the Lamb of God,
Who sacrificed His blood to purchase people from
every tribe.
Worthy of praise, worthy of honor, worthy of thanks-
giving, worthy of worship,
Worthy of my whole heart, worthy of my whole body,
worthy of my whole mind, worthy of all my strength.[26]

All the while, the young men of the family sat in the window frame, watched, and listened. In the shadow of their scrutiny, I felt awed by the faith and courage of the Afghan women around me. They knew the danger, and yet they worshiped.

I imagine Father God, receiving our worship, delighted in His children.

After we sang, one of the men of the family entered the room where we were sitting. He demanded to see the book, the New Testament from which we'd read.

I watched and prayed as he sat in the corner of the room

reading pages of the book. I had no idea what he would do. It was clear that the women of the household were also nervous. Our conversation continued, but stiffly.

Finally, after about fifteen minutes, the man shoved the book into his pocket and stood up from the floor.

I held my breath.

He nodded to no one in particular and declared his judgment: "It's good." With that, he left. The young men who'd been watching and listening in the window also left, and so our weekly gatherings continued.

Someday, I may see those men in heaven. I shall certainly see some of the women. I expect to see the young returnee from Iran who asked for a copy of the book of Jesus. And perhaps I shall see that mother who lost seven sons in one Taliban bomb. I hope I see some of the men and women from the village who asked me not to return. I'm sure I'll see my woman friend who lives there.

Why does God call us to dangerous places? Because we can't touch people, heal their bodies, hand them a book, or worship and pray with them from 7,400 miles away. Love and truth takes on flesh and walks the earth, and He does so within us.

We who go, fragile, stumbling human beings, each recognized an invitation to walk with Christ in a dangerous place and responded, trusting the One leading us.

DISCUSSION GUIDE

Chapter 6: They Have to Hear, See, Touch

1. Was there a time in your life when you experienced the love of God through the actions of a person or group of people? What was that like for you?

2. When have you shown God's love to someone through your actions? What was that like for you?

3. Consider 2 Corinthians 5:20. What does it mean to you to be Christ's ambassador?

4. Read Colossians 1:27. Write out the verse and read it aloud. How do you carry Christ in you to those He's put in your life?

5. How does God bless His people when they suffer persecution? Take a few moments to pray for the persecuted church or journal a prayer on their behalf.

Chapter 7

FOLLOWING HIS CALL

Our very question invites God to reveal His heart, "for even the Son of Man came not to be served but to serve, and to give his life as a ransom for many." —Mark 10:45

Each person who has walked with Christ in a dangerous place speaks of a call, an invitation from the Spirit that moves within him or her.

One man writes:

I would never have come to work in Afghanistan if I hadn't been sure about God's clear calling. I believe everyone should be obedient to the specific calling God gives, not necessarily because there is blessing involved, but mainly because I want to acknowledge who God is to me and what He has done for me.
—Werner Groenewald[1]

This Christ-follower and his two children were killed in Kabul, Afghanistan, just hours after he sent me these words. Werner had lived in the country for years and clearly knew the dangers. Still, he and his family stayed in the place where God had called them.

For some, the call is clear and dramatic. For others it grows more slowly, unfolding as we take each step of obedience. One Christ-follower might experience an awareness of a desire to serve God in a particular place or way. Another finds himself burdened for a specific need like food, clean water, honest business, or putting a stop to human trafficking.

One woman recounts her story of following the Spirit's lead in the following words:

> For us, the calling grew and changed as we walked, endeavoring to follow. For me it came first as a call to assist the poor. I guess back then, with the images I had seen, Africa seemed to be the place. But as my first opportunity to spend three months somewhere in the third world came, God closed doors to Africa and presented an open door to go to the Northwest Frontier Province of Pakistan. There, God exposed me to poor Afghan refugees, Pashtuns. So my call narrowed to Pashtuns. Others in leadership encouraged us to go to India instead, but in God's wisdom, He closed those doors. Finally as we prepared to go back to Pakistan, we were asked if we would consider Afghanistan. As

our call at that point was more to the Pashtun people
than to a locality, we moved across the border to Afghanistan to work with Pashtuns.
—An aid worker in Afghanistan

For this woman, God's call unfolded over time as she and
later her family walked in obedience and faithfulness to the
steps before them.

Other Christ-followers come to the end of their careers and
find themselves considering the desire to offer their professional
skills for those who are underserved.

One couple spent almost twenty
years running a hospital in Haiti.
When it was time to hand over the
hospital to Haitian administrators,
they consecrated their lives to God
anew and said, in effect, We'll go
anywhere You want us to. Within a
year, they were offering their experience and skills in a war-torn Asian
country.

Another couple sent their children to college, watched them settle
into their careers, and responded to a
quiet, germinating dream. They, too,
followed God's call to a dangerous place.

WHEN WE RESPOND to the call, we offer our lives to God as a living sacrifice. We may still find ourselves in college, at work, or quietly raising our children, yet something within us has changed. We are counting the cost and recognizing Christ as worth the most treasured gifts we can give Him.

An American couple sensed God's call and brought their

five small children with them to live in Afghanistan. The mother writes:

> We moved our family to a place, not out of desire for adventure but out of a desire to be obedient to God calling us there. While those around us tried to work their way to heaven, I was daily reminded how thankful I am that I serve a real and living God who loves me and wants a relationship with me. —A mother in Afghanistan

For some, the call comes in their teenage or young adult years. One young woman sensed the Lord drawing her to Iraq. While still a college student, she spent two summers in northern Iraq, teaching English to Kurdish young adults. Now, she dreams of returning to the community she's grown to love.

Another woman writes of her journey to a dangerous place.

> Somewhere along the way of growing up, I had met a great God who reached down and changed my life forever by His promise of redemption, and His gift of perfect love. The opportunity came when I watched as a senior in college two airplanes collide into the historic twin towers, and the stories of Afghanistan began to explode across the media. My heart broke for the struggles that the nation had endured, and I prayed

a simple prayer, "Use me there Lord." —An aid worker
in Afghanistan

Each of these individuals and many others experienced a
call and responded because they knew God and what He's done
for us.

The journey to a dangerous place always begins in our hearts
first. From the moment we sense God's call to walk with Him in
a dangerous place, we face the possibility that responding may
cost us our lives. This is a sobering reality that challenges us to
consider our willingness to not only live for the gospel, but to
suffer and die for it as well.

When we respond to the call, we offer our lives to God as a
living sacrifice.[2] We may still find ourselves in college, at work,
or quietly raising our children, yet something within us has
changed. We are counting the cost and recognizing Christ as
worth the most treasured gifts we can give Him.

Our very willingness to go is an act of spiritual worship[3] offered as a precious gift to the God we love. We give back to Him
what He's given to us in the first place. He calls and we respond.
We trust that no matter what happens, we are in God's hands.
We respond, willing to suffer and die, but not seeking death for
its own sake.

Shortly after an aid worker was kidnapped and killed in
Afghanistan, I met another worker who seemed to glory in the
possibility of martyrdom. She told me over cups of tea how she
so desired to give her life for the sake of the gospel.

At the time, I experienced confusion. Does God want us to seek martyrdom? It didn't make sense. Since then, we've lost more than twenty workers in Afghanistan, all brutally killed. Each loss has filled me with sorrow and heartache. A friend in Afghanistan articulated it well when she wrote, "Losing one friend is bad enough. Seeing over a dozen murdered does something deep in your soul."

We don't go to a dangerous place so that we can be martyred. The same friend I quoted above writes:

> Our calling as Christians is to life . . . and life abundant. That is the first thing we need to get right, not an obsession, fear or glorification of martyrdom (just look into jihad if you want to see where glorifying the death of martyrs will take us). One of my mentors early in the field[4] said to me, "When you come here you have to face that you might die, then get on with living here." That is so important—how we live in dangerous places, freely, boldly, wisely, lovingly, full of compassion and energy and clinging fast to Jesus—who is with us and has gone ahead of us. I would be very hesitant of being up for suffering for suffering's sake . . . and yet we have lost a theology of suffering in the current Western church. We are very uncomfortable with it.

There's so much wisdom in her words. We are called first to Christ and, in Christ, to abundant life. We seek to live fully and love deeply, "clinging fast to Jesus." The risk of losing our lives for the sake of the gospel should not stop us from going, nor should the desire to become martyrs compel us. Instead, we go "because Jesus is there and it is a privilege to serve Him and love people in His name in those places with Him."

Still, martyrdom is a possibility we must consider. Like the apostle Paul, we face threats against our lives with mixed desires. Paul wrote,

> It is my eager expectation and hope that I will not be at all ashamed, but that with full courage now as always Christ will be honored in my body, whether by life or by death. For to me to live is Christ, and to die is gain. If I am to live in the flesh, that means fruitful labor for me. Yet which I shall choose I cannot tell. I am hard pressed between the two. My desire is to depart and be with Christ, for that is far better. But to remain in the flesh is more necessary on your account.[5]

We know that those who've been brutally killed for the gospel in Afghanistan, Yemen, Libya, and a hundred other places are now safely in the arms of Christ. We also know the pain and loss experienced by those who remain alive. We hold within our hearts a deep desire to be fully with Christ and a deep love for the world into which He's called us.

One man writes of his experience in facing death:

One night in Nooristan, Afghanistan, I had to spend a night sleeping outdoors with a small group of coworkers. Approximately a hundred meters up the trail, a group of men also set up camp. They were notorious robbers and killers. The Afghans in our group were terrified. When they said that, with such conviction, I believed them wholeheartedly. A deep joy gripped me so I could not stop smiling. In my heart and mind, I was convinced that I would finally meet Jesus face-to-face. I was so excited that I had a hard time falling asleep. I prayed, "Lord, I am so excited to meet You in a few hours. But, if You want people to experience Your love in this area, nobody else will come up here again if I am killed. I am excited about seeing You, but people here need You." The next day I was a little disappointed . . . but continued up the valley . . . KNOWING my life was in God's hands, not in any man's. To this day I am convinced about that. It gives me peace beyond what the world can give.

—An aid worker in Afghanistan.

The moment we say yes to God—yes, I'm willing to go; yes, I'm willing to die—we begin our journey. At this point, the dangerous place in which we're walking is in our hearts. We find ourselves praying for the people God has drawn us to. We share our hopes and fears with others in our lives. We wrestle with the cost and make sacrificial decisions in obedience to the call. We place our hand in Christ's hand and walk with Him, trusting He will lead us every step of the way. This is the season of discernment, of clarifying the call, and of preparing to go. We may walk this season for several years.

I first sensed the call to walk with Christ in Afghanistan in late 2000. I boarded a plane four years later. During those years, I explored the call and prepared to go. My journey included prayer, journaling, research, the wise counsel of spiritually mature advisors, and a myriad of small and large decisions. Along the way, God both prepared me to go and welcomed me into His heart for the people of Afghanistan.

BY THE TIME I actually moved to Afghanistan, I knew with absolute confidence that Christ had called me to that country. At the time, I told my friends in America, "Jesus has invited me to walk with Him in Afghanistan and I'm just crazy in love with Him enough to do it!"

By the time I actually moved to Afghanistan, I knew with absolute confidence that Christ had called me to that country. At the time, I told my friends in America, "Jesus has invited me to walk with Him in Afghanistan, and I'm just crazy in love with Him enough to do it!"

I also knew a great deal about the situation in Afghanistan and was ready to quickly enter the culture. I had learned enough language before I went to engage in the most basic conversations and had determined how I would serve the Afghan people.

Most important, through those years of discernment and preparation, I had grown in my understanding of my own needs and weaknesses and had strengthened my spiritual disciplines. Those lessons proved critical as I lived and worked in a dangerous place.

Over the years, I've had the privilege of walking with others while they discerned God's call on their lives and prepared to live and work in a dangerous place. Many come to me with a dream wrapped in doubts, fears, and unanswered questions.

One of the first things I ask them to do is to invite others into their journey. This is a hard step. Most Western adults want their questions answered. "Oh, you want to go overseas? What will you do? Who will you work with? When are you going?"

Those who are called but who are still in the discernment-and-preparation phase struggle with such questions. We live in a society that values self-determination and decisiveness. We love a well-formed and articulated plan. But the journey to the field is one that must be led by God if it is to be taken at all. And God does not value self-determination or decisiveness. Instead, He values sensitivity to His Spirit, patience, and obedience.

Responding to the call and preparing for the field are part of the journey. This season is necessary for those who go and for those who prepare to go but realize later that God is leading them elsewhere. For those of us who sense the call, our role is to walk this part of the journey with Christ, trusting He is leading us along the way.

When we love those who sense the call, our role is to pray for them, encourage them, and help them discern God's leading with open hearts and hands. We enter their journey, not knowing where it will lead, but trusting God for those we love. We offer our gifts to those whom God is calling to a dangerous place.

Often I've heard young adults complain of how long it takes to move from the initial call to actually going. Many speak of "waiting" and express frustration with the slow pace of their journeys and their lack of clarity about where they will go, when they will leave, and with whom they will work.

God is the One who is doing a good work within us. Sometimes we're able to see and name what He's doing. For me, it was easy to recognize the outward steps of the journey: leaving my career, selling my house, joining an overseas organization, acquiring my letters of invitation and visa, buying tickets. Those were important steps, and each included a loss and a gain. The losses demanded grieving and the gains, celebrations.

But the most important work was what Christ was doing within me. In many ways, He was stripping away my idealistic dreams, false motivations, and my own sense of control and self-determination. He was developing within me a deeper sensitivity to His Spirit's gentle leading. He was also filling my pockets with gifts, most of which I didn't recognize until I faced situations on the field that required the treasures He'd given me along the way.

The season of waiting is not waiting at all. It's more like gestation, a quiet growth where Christ, through His Spirit, His Scriptures, and His people prepares us for the journey ahead. It's a sacred season and every bit as much a part of the journey as that which is actually lived on the field.

Sometimes this season of the journey ends at an airport terminal. When it does, we celebrate the joy of walking into Christ's call on our lives.

I recall one young couple from the United States whom I met in Dubai. They were moving, with their small child, to Afghanistan. God had birthed the call in each years earlier. For the wife, the call came first as a teenager when she met an overseas worker at her church. For the husband, the call came while he was in college, attending a conference.

When they met each other, they shared their calls with each other and looked to Christ to fulfill the dreams He'd given them. That was ten years before I met them in Dubai. Along the way, they had graduated college, married, worked, and grown closer to Jesus and each other.

Three years before I met them, they sensed it was time and began intentionally preparing for their journey to a dangerous place. They invited their family, loved ones, church community, and trusted advisors to walk with them. Finally, they loaded their luggage, their small son, and all the gifts Christ had given them into a taxi and headed for the airport.

When I met them in Dubai, they were full of excitement and gratefulness. Their joy was infectious, and I felt privileged to share it with them.

For others, the journey ends in disappointment. One young couple had their hearts set on moving to Afghanistan. As they were preparing, the husband was diagnosed with an illness that required constant medication and ongoing testing. In one shocking medical appointment, their dreams of walking with Christ in a dangerous place were dashed.

They found themselves full of confusion. "Did we misunderstand Your call?" "Were we pursuing our own ends?" "What do we do now?"

Both experiences call us to deep trust.

We must believe that Christ actually called both of these dear couples to a dangerous place. We choose to be confident that during their seasons of discernment and preparation, God was filling them with good and perfect gifts[6] for their blessings and His glory. Most fundamentally, we must trust that Christ loves both of these couples and has a plan and purpose for their lives.[7] In each experience, we lean on the scriptural promise "that God causes all things to work together for good to those who love God, to those who are called according to His purpose."[8]

With the ones who climb aboard an airplane, we celebrate. With those who face a closed door, we grieve. All are part of God's call to a dangerous place, and all are transformed through the journey.

The experience of a closed door can be confusing, but it's not without precedent. The great apostle Paul faced a closed door to preaching the gospel in Asia.[9] His story goes on to tell us that "when they [Paul and his companions] had come up to Mysia, they attempted to go into Bithynia, but the Spirit of Jesus did not allow them."[10] Later, Paul went to Troas, but when he arrived, he experienced a call to Macedonia.[11]

For those of us, including myself, who prefer well-articulated plans, such journeys with Christ can leave us full of questions and doubts. Yet it's in these places of disappointment where we develop patience, obedience, and a deepening sensitivity to God's Spirit.

One couple spent several years preparing to move to Pakistan. When the time finally arrived, they boarded a series of planes that took them to Islamabad. They arrived in the capital of Pakistan on September 11, 2001. Their team members met them at the airport, but instead of loading their baggage into a taxi, they led them onto another plane. Their life with Christ in Pakistan would have to wait.

We would prefer a sense of competence, the strength of our own agency, yet Christ calls us to follow Him and trust that He, the Good Shepherd, will lead us well.

When Christ calls us to walk with Him in a dangerous place, our responsibility is to respond with our hands and hearts open to wherever He leads us. For some, the call leads us to the places of which we've dreamed. For others, it may lead us someplace else entirely. Here, we experience a strong sense of confirmation that allows us to live in the place to which God has called us.

I remember the first time I stepped down on Afghan soil. I had crossed the river from Tajikistan in a small boat and stood on the bank on the Afghan side. In those moments, while men with Kalashnikovs checked my passport, I experienced a deep sense of knowing *this is it. This is where I belong.* It was firm, solid, and unshakable.

Over time, as I walked the streets, visited Afghans in their homes, breathed the Afghan dust, and listened to the long calls of prayer amplified from the local mosques, that sense of knowing grew stronger.

I didn't know where the journey would lead me. None of us do. And once again, I recall James and John, two fishermen who left their nets to follow Jesus.[12] They had no idea where their journey with Jesus would take them and, in fact, carried expectations that would not be realized.[13] Still, they followed.

When we go to a dangerous place, we go with our hopes and dreams in one hand and the other tucked safely in the hand of Jesus, our guide and companion. We carry in our pockets every skill, talent, and gift that God has already given us. Some we are aware of, some we are not. We find them when we need them and discover that God has been faithful to prepare us for whatever situation we face.

We respond to God's call in the community of others: our friends, our family members, our trusted advisors, and our faith communities. These others are also part of the journey and experience the blessings and challenges, the joys and losses of following Christ to a dangerous place.

DISCUSSION GUIDE

Chapter 7: Following His Call

1. Consider Philippians 1:20–24. What do you think Paul meant by verse 21, "For me to live is Christ and to die is gain"?

2. Read Romans 12:1. What are you willing to give to God?

3. Has God ever called you to do something difficult? What was that like for you?

4. Consider Jeremiah 29:11. Many view this verse as a promise that this life will be free of pain. Instead, what promise do you see in verses 11–13 in spite of the inevitable hardships of this earthly life?

5. Read Mark 10:35–45. Write out verse 45 and journal what it means to you that Jesus "came not to be
   served, but to serve." How can you seek to walk as
   Jesus walked in His humility and servant heart?

Chapter 8

SENDING OUR FRIENDS AND FAMILIES

"When one of us follows Christ into a dangerous place, our friends, families, and faith communities go with us. There is a cost to all of us."

A young couple approached me in the hallway of an American college. "We feel like God is calling us to Afghanistan, but we don't think our parents want us to go. What should we do?" They recognized that their journey with Jesus to a dangerous place included their parents.

Immediately, I remembered a conversation I'd had with the parents of a worker who was living in a remote and unstable village in the mountains of Afghanistan. When I spoke with that mother and father, I heard voices of deep faith and equally deep fear. I felt the heartbeat of a love so strong it ached to embrace their daughter and protect her from all the evils in the world and yet celebrated the journey of that same child with Jesus.

When we go to a dangerous place, we take our parents, our siblings, and all who love us into the lands where God has called us. They may never get their passports and climb on an airplane, but they go with us nonetheless.

One of my closest friends in America checked the Afghan news feeds every morning. She learned the map of Afghanistan, the locations of cities, villages, and mountain ranges. She looked at my pictures and learned the names of my friends, both foreign and Afghan. Each day, she prayed for me and for the people I loved.

She was not alone. All over the world, families and friends have breathed the dust of foreign lands, learned the names and faces of people they will never meet in this life, and held each one before the God who loves. These, too, go to dangerous places.

They awaken in the middle of the night to pray. They write encouraging emails, read stories they find difficult to understand, and share the journeys of their loved ones with neighbors and strangers. Each day, with all their hopes and fears, they lean into God. For many, the journey is full of heartache, gratefulness, and loneliness. Many dedicated their children to the Lord and then stood weeping as those same children disappeared through airport security or packed their bags and moved into some forgotten inner-city neighborhood.

One mother spoke to me about her daily battle with fear. Each morning and throughout each day, she found herself praying, offering herself and her son to God, begging for strength and for her son's protection, aching for her son to come home, and breathing her gratefulness that he had chosen Christ above all. She spoke of her pain and fear and of the strength and encouragement she received from Jesus, His Spirit, the Scriptures, and His people.

ALL OVER THE WORLD, families and friends have breathed the dust of foreign lands, learned the names and faces of people they will never meet in this life, and held each one before the God who loves. These, too, go to dangerous places.

Another mother recalled the long days when her daughter gathered supplies and packed her gear. She described her heartache when her daughter boarded the plane that would carry her into danger. She wrote about her fear, the ache in her heart, and the comfort she received through God's people.

When my own daughter left to go to the field, I was very uncertain as to its effect upon my daughter's safety and health. In prayer that night, I prayed, releasing the fear that gripped me, having to let her go into God's hand. I felt like she was being torn out of me. I had no choice but to trust God for her safety, and her life. I sobbed from the depth of my being, pouring out to Jesus all my complete lack of control. I depended on the prayers of many others to keep her safe, as I could hardly pray for her even while she was gone. God comforted me the day of her travel. A friend met me at

my home after my husband and I saw our daughter off
on the plane. My friend was there to encourage us that
God was with my daughter and would stay beside her.
—JA, a mother[1]

When I hear the stories of parents who've watched their
children go off to dangerous places for the sake of the gospel, I
recall a poem by Martin Bell. The last lines read:

Today other mommas are holding their children.
Children who will grow up and follow where He leads
them.
God have mercy, and comfort on all the mommas
Of children who change the world.[2]

I'm reminded of another mother, young, her infant child in
her arms. I can almost see her, her husband at her side, walking through the crowds of Jerusalem. In obedience to God, the
couple carries with them two small birds, their humble offering.[3] An old man approaches them. He lifts the child in his own
hands and offers a deep prayer of faith and celebration.[4]

Then the old man turns to the young mother and speaks
words that would haunt any mother's heart: "Behold, this child
is appointed for the fall and rising of many in Israel, and for a
sign that is opposed (and a sword will pierce through your own
soul also), so that thoughts from many hearts may be revealed."[5]

I imagine young Mary and her husband, Joseph, watching and listening, wondering at the man's words. Perhaps Mary pondered those words in her heart, along with the stories of the shepherds that first night when her Son was born.[6] Perhaps she recalled them, years later, when she stood on Golgotha at the foot of a Roman cross and watched in horror as her beloved Son died.

> God have mercy, and comfort on all the mommas
> Of children who change the world.[7]

Those who love those who are called also receive an invitation to walk closely with Jesus. Some embrace that invitation, lean into Christ, and find themselves growing deeper and stronger through the journey.

A mother from Texas spoke to me of the love she saw in her son and daughter-in-law for the people of the dangerous land in which they worked, and how their love stirred deep compassion within her own heart.

Another woman wrote of the ways in which her own faith journey came into clearer focus and purity. She saw her son's commitment and sacrifice and found herself yearning more deeply for the kingdom of God in her own life and community. My own mother has spoken to me many times of her deepening faith as daily she committed me into the hands of Christ.

One mother wrote of how her trust in God grew through the experience of sharing her young daughter's journey.

When my daughter graduated from our homeschool, her first desire was to go on the field. Prayer and seeking opened a door for ministry in Muslim North Africa. Although the country to which God called her was a "closed" country—illegal to preach the gospel, and my daughter was only 18 at the time—we felt God's peace that this was the call that He had on her life. She is, after all, not ours but belongs wholly to her Beloved. Though the dangers of this assignment were real, His grace and His hunger for the people of this Muslim nation to know Him were more real. So our hearts were at rest as we released her to be Jesus in this dark place. Our trust in Him grew as we watched and prayed from afar. —A mother

Some parents, siblings, and dear friends visit their loved ones on the field. The day I moved to Afghanistan, I traveled into the country with a mother from the States. Along the way, she shared her nervousness, her fear, and her deep pride in her daughter's journey.

Another couple traveled into Afghanistan to visit an adult daughter who was working in a remote community. They agonized over how to pack, what clothes to wear, and how they would ever manage to endure the long trip.

Their visit brought strength, joy, and deep encouragement to their daughter, but that wasn't all. The national members of their daughter's community embraced these parents and welcomed them into their homes. They delighted in the opportunity to get to know such precious family members.

In the end, the couple returned to America deeply grateful for the opportunity to visit their daughter and to get to know the people she had grown to love so deeply. They both experienced and shared God's love in a very dangerous land and found themselves the richer for it.

One American father went to Afghanistan to visit his daughter and get to know her friends. He met good and decent Afghans who loved and cared for his adult child. They shared meals and stories, laughter, joy, and hope for the country his family had been called to love.

Some months later, that same father returned to Kabul. His second trip was full of heartache and loss. He and the Kabul community buried his daughter in the one cemetery in Afghanistan that could receive her remains. The man's daughter had been killed with a group of other aid workers while providing medical assistance to remote communities in the mountains of Afghanistan. On this second visit, the father shared his grief with Afghan and foreign men and women who knew both him and his daughter.

FOR EVERY ONE of us who actually boards a plane, others go with us in heart, mind, and spirit. Each pays a price and experiences Christ in the journey. For some, watching a beloved friend leave is frightening and heartbreaking.

At his daughter's memorial service in America, this father

said, "I'm so grateful for her, the impact she's had on our lives. We just want to give thanks to God for her." Somehow, in his sorrow and loss, he experienced the joy and comfort of Christ's love.

None of us lives our lives with Christ alone. Each is embedded in a colorful tapestry of interpersonal relationships. When one of us follows Christ into a dangerous place, our friends, families, and faith communities go with us. There is a cost to all of us.

When I first told the members of my small group that I sensed God calling me to Afghanistan, they immediately rejected the idea. "No. It's too dangerous." The prospect of one of their own going to such a place was unthinkable.

Over time, my small group members and prayer partners settled into the call and embraced the journey. They prayed with me and for me. They helped me discern Christ's leading and navigate the myriad of decisions I faced as I extricated my life from America and moved toward the field. When the time came, they donated their resources to make the journey possible.

Coworkers, friends, and members of my broader community also assisted. They offered their support, prayers, and encouragement. Many shared in my journey as it unfolded each day. They read my email updates, connected with me via Skype, looked at my pictures, and gave of their finances to support the work we were doing.

For every one of us who actually boards a plane, others go with us in heart, mind, and spirit. Each pays a price and experiences Christ in the journey. For some, watching a beloved friend leave is frightening and heartbreaking. One woman shared of the cost of loving someone who went to a dangerous place in these words:

> When I had a close friend going into the field, answering the call to a dangerous location, I was completely overwhelmed, unable to accompany her to the airport. The night before she left, after a prayer gathering for her, she and I walked down the driveway. I feared our friendship would change forever because she was going to answer a call to carry Jesus to the world, even if it was unsafe for her. I didn't know if she would ever come back. I knew she would be visible to the enemy because of her eyes, and height, and her fearless love for others and for Jesus. I knew others and I would pray for her safety. Beyond that we could not control her safety, nor could she. So, though I did not totally trust God to protect her, my only safe place was to trust that God would bring her home safely. When I stepped into the street, I felt as if I stepped off a cliff, with incredible uncertainty of the future. —JA

When we love deeply, our hearts are laced together. The tearing apart wounds us; in our pain and fear, we lean into Christ who alone can comfort us. The journey isn't easy, but Christ is faithful and His mercies are new each and every morning.[8]

Sometimes sharing the journey is full of joy. One woman wrote:

> From the first time I heard a woman from our community speak about her calling from God and love for the Afghanistan women, I knew it was God calling her to go and live the gospel of Jesus Christ to others. She has inspired and encouraged me in my faith. There were so many answers to prayer along her journey, and it was a privilege to pray for God to take care of her and rejoice with her as she saw God's presence and transforming power each day! —JA

For some, their involvement with those who go starts off small, but deepens over time. They, too, answer a call, an invitation from Christ that changes their perspective on the world around them and on what they have to give to God's kingdom work. One man wrote:

> Quite honestly, it started out as just helping the friend of a friend with a vision that was doing something that I could never imagine doing. Maybe a little vicarious living or substituting money for action at the start, but it just can't stay that way for long. Learning about the "foreignness" of another culture, especially one hostile to the Gospel, moves you quickly into areas in your own life that follow a parallel track, although a much

safer one. You find yourself starting to think about the culture you live in and how often you make assumptions about what the people around you think and feel. You begin to separate country and cultural norms from your faith, getting closer to the heart of what it means to be a believer, and being sensitive to the worldview of those you come into contact with. You also begin to realize how much of a support network is needed to place and sustain someone in those dangerous areas, and how important it is to be a part of that support structure, no matter how small you may think your own contribution is. —WN

Many experience growth in their own service to Christ.

Some friends and family members find creative ways to offer their hands, even from afar. Several American-based friends of mine collected small bottles of lotion, shampoo and conditioner, and bars of soap. These they sent that my friends and I might share their gifts with Afghan neighbors.

A group of American women bought colorful fabric remnants and sewed small gift bags. On the

LOVING SOMEONE LIVING in dangerous places has a sobering effect on my relationship with God, because I have a personal concern for their safety, while understanding the totality and reality of what His calling entails, even if it be death for Christ. It quickens in me the desire to seek opportunities to love people with His love, pray by faith for the results, and know the glorious end is in God's hands. —SP field, a foreign friend packed some of the bags with juice boxes, first aid supplies, nail polish, and small notes of cash. She shared her bags with street beggars and watched the delight of women and children as they received their small gifts.

Another coworker in Afghanistan filled bags with reading glasses and shared them with students in her literacy project. Now those colorful gift bags, sewn by the hands of American women, are all over Afghanistan.

One man collected and shipped welding safety supplies to the field. Others mailed wound-care bandages, burn ointment, and antibiotic salve. A group of women crocheted baby hats for Afghan mothers who participated in training groups. A man shipped over thermal shirts and thick socks for orphan boys. Each offered what they had to give and celebrated the opportunity to share.

One woman wrote of her experience in the following story:

When my friend was in Afghanistan, I was able to send packages with little things like pretty napkins and snacks for parties she had with the women, colorful posters for the kids at school. I also sent some simple items my friend missed from home, like animal crackers.

Truly, there is no material thing you could give me, no fame, no success, no recognition by man that could ever bring as much joy as knowing that I could send a tiny bit of comfort or beauty over there in hopes that

God's love would be more manifest in that war-torn
land. —GC

Each person who uses his or her hands to bless distant
neighbors experiences the joy and grace of sharing Christ's love
across miles and cultures. Their example reminds me of Paul's
words to the elders of Ephesus: "In everything I showed you
that by working hard in this manner you must help the weak and
remember the words of the Lord Jesus, that He Himself said, 'It
is more blessed to give than to receive.'"[9]

Sometimes parents, friends, and family members welcome
their loved ones home only to discover that their children, siblings, and friends have changed along the way. They struggle to
understand and respond.

We who go return forever changed by our journeys. Virtually all of us return grieving those we've left behind. Some of us
reenter our home countries carrying the stress of the traumas
we've experienced directly or indirectly.

One returning man told me about leaping out of his bed at
the sound of a garbage truck. Another told me of the panic she
felt when a hospital helicopter swept her heart back to the field.
I still tense at the sight of groups of men clustered on the street.

A few years ago, after visiting a dear friend who had been
kidnapped and released, I returned to the States full of confusion and sorrow. My closest friend sat with me as I sobbed. Her
wordless presence was the greatest gift I could receive.

One young man returned to the States after a season of

working at an orphanage in Mozambique. He de-boarded the airplane and immediately faced the commercial excess of Christmas in America. Every emotion within him clashed with chaotic incongruity. His family listened as he struggled and loved him through it. Their response, also, was a gift.

Often we return to our homes only to find ourselves lost, disoriented, and confused; our minds and hearts are still deeply attached to the countries in which we've served. We miss our friends, foods, and customs. We look at the world with different eyes and struggle to make sense of home countries that have changed while we were gone.

Our families and friends walk with us in our struggles. They seek God's grace and wisdom. Those who find Christ's grace welcome and love our hearts and minds home.

When I think of those who've welcomed me so well, I'm reminded of the apostle Paul's words: "I thank my God in all my remembrance of you, always in every prayer of mine for you all making my prayer with joy, because of your partnership in the gospel from the first day until now."[10]

Those who love people who are called to a dangerous place share in every aspect of the journey and find themselves growing deeper in Christ through the joys and sorrows they experience. But it's not only families and friends who walk the path. It's also church communities who are invited to share the journey.

DISCUSSION GUIDE

Chapter 8: Sending Our Friends and Families

1. Do you know that God is calling someone you love to a dangerous place? If not, can you imagine it? What emotions does that stir in you?

2. Read Philippians 4:6–7 aloud. How might you embrace Christ's peace even while those you love are in danger?

3. How might you encourage someone else whose loved ones are in danger? If you are going through this book in a small group, pray for those who have loved ones in danger.

4. Who has helped you in difficult seasons in your life? How did they help?

5. Read Acts 20:35. We're told that Jesus said, "It is more blessed to give than to receive." Those words have been quoted so often it's easy to take them for granted. Who might God be calling you to help now?

Chapter 9

HOW CAN WE SEND OUR PEOPLE?

"When the church stops sending her children to the world, she begins to die." —Christian Leader, Ghana

In the early days of the modern missions movement, nineteenth-century men and women bought one-way tickets to Africa and carried their coffins with them. They didn't expect to return home.

A twenty-first-century Ghanaian Christian leader shared their stories from his own grateful perspective. The first missionaries who reached his shores died almost immediately. More came. They, too, died. Still, more came. Some were killed violently and others were carried away by disease, yet more came. Today, there are more than 12 million Christians in Ghana and only God knows how many Ghanaian Christians are already in heaven.

These are our brothers and sisters, our spiritual siblings. They share with us the "one faith, one baptism, one God and Father of all."[1] They also share with us the unique gifts that Christ has given them.[2]

Both the table of the Lord in heaven and the Communion of the saints here on earth are richer, fuller, and more complete thanks to those men and women who left their homes, ready to die for the name of the Lord Jesus.[3]

Behind those nineteenth-century missionaries were church communities, family members, and beloved friends who both wept at their departure and released their loved ones to God. They, too, share in the fruits of the sacrifice.

How could they do it? How can we?

For most of our churches, missions is a program: a few lines on the bulletin, a rarely updated page on the website, and an add-on to the budget after their members have supported the on-site ministries and facilities of the church local. The stories of refugees in the Middle East and disease-wracked populations in West Africa fall from the evening news. If we're paying attention, they make it to our Sunday morning prayer requests, but in my own experience, most tangible help is offered by individuals rather than by our faith communities.[4]

Orphanages, schools, Bible colleges, hospitals, and clinics—all expressions of God's people being the people of God in a suffering world—compete with our desire for a new sound system for the sanctuary, new carpeting, and that extra staff member to coordinate adult ministries.

Sending people to the world is hard. Sending them to dangerous places is even harder.

Why should we do it?

A Ghanaian Christian leader articulated a truth that shook me to the core: "When the church stops sending her children to the world, she begins to die." Sending is the heart of God, who sent His own Son into the world.

Most of us who go with Christ to a dangerous place are first members of a local church. In our churches, we grow in faith and wisdom. We find love, encouragement, and guidance. Often, when we sense the call to a dangerous place, we share our fears and excitement with our church leaders.

Some church leaders fully embrace the call. They pray for their members, counsel, guide, encourage, and celebrate. They assist their members in preparing for the journey, anoint or lay hands on them to confirm the work, support and stay connected with them while they're gone, and welcome them home with open arms.

My own journey was graced with a supporting church. Several months after I sensed God calling me to Afghanistan, I made an appointment to speak with one of our church pastors. I shared my thoughts with him and wondered, out loud, if God was calling me and if I could really follow Him to the other side of the world. I hoped my pastor would help me walk the journey, no matter where it led.

Over the next several years, I met monthly with my pastor. He spent hours listening to me, helping me discern God's leading, providing me with resources, talking through my decisions, and praying with and for me. Between our meetings, I often emailed him with different ideas I was considering. He always responded quickly. His email quote below provides just a glimpse of his approach to sending one of his own out to a dangerous place.

> When you are ready, I would love to talk with you about it. In the meantime, I will just pray blessing on the good work He is doing in you and continue to ask that He will clarify and strengthen His sense of anointing and calling for you. You are a blessing! —MS

My pastor's role in my journey was invaluable. I might have made it to the field without his assistance, but I certainly wouldn't have been as confident, prepared, or supported. I am forever grateful to God for my pastor's willingness to invest so much in God's call on my life.

The cost of sending includes not only time, but also the presence of church members. Most church leaders work very hard at developing programs and activities to both welcome visitors into their fellowship and involve congregants in the life of the church. They don't usually look for opportunities to send people away! But some hear God's heartbeat, accept the sacrifice, and send their own.

One church sent their youth leader along with his wife and child to a dangerous place. Another sent one of their worship leaders. Yet another sent their outreach committee chair. These churches lost people who contributed greatly to the lives of their communities.

My own pastor jokingly hinted at the mix of blessing and loss when he wrote:

> So I ain't writin' no reference letter if it means you are
> leaving any time soon! The letter only comes when
> you promise to have a replacement in place before you
> go anywhere long term. Only kidding—sort of. —MS

It is hard to send people when it means losing them.

In addition to these challenges, churches are also called upon to invest their limited financial resources in those who once donated such resources. They pray and wonder how God will provide.

Church leaders also know that the work of those who go, unlike the work of those who stay at home, will never add new members to their communities. Offering a congregant to God's call is a sacrifice, particularly when God calls one of their own to a dangerous place.

"IN THE MIDST OF our sorrow, we were reminded that the greatest loss would be for us to hold back from following Christ because we are trying to save our lives, when Jesus and His gospel is of supreme value to us."
—A church leader who lost members to violence in Afghanistan

Some churches have paid the ultimate price. They've stood

stunned and abashed as loved ones from their church communities have been kidnapped or killed on the field. Grief and shock sweeps through their congregations. Their communities are forever changed. A church leader in Illinois shared her community's experience in losing beloved members to violence in Afghanistan.

> The Sunday after two of our members were killed in Afghanistan, our pastor, Colin Smith, spoke words of both comfort and challenge to our church. He reminded us that the great question for our church at this time of shock and grief was not "Why did this happen?" but "Is it worth it?" Could we say that Jesus Christ is worth more than the world and more than our lives? Our members believed this. The question is, did we?
> In the midst of our sorrow, we were reminded that the greatest loss would be for us to hold back from following Christ because we are trying to save our lives, when Jesus and His gospel is of supreme value to us. Our church has really rallied around the family of our lost members who, of course, are still mourning and miss their husband and father. But, in the face of the realities of what the cost can be in following Jesus, we are praying that God would raise up hundreds of men and women who will say, *"Jesus Christ is worth more to me than all the world, and following Christ is worth any*

price, even if it costs me my life." —Linda Green, The
Orchard Evangelical Free Church

For that community, the dangers became brutally real. They
grieved and surely still do, yet they count Christ as worth it.

For some churches, the opportunity to partner with an
overseas worker is an answer to prayer. On September 11, 2001,
a pastor of a rural church gathered with his stunned and heartbroken congregation to pray and grieve. They asked God to
show them how they could respond to the brutal violence of
that day. Several years later they welcomed a worker headed for
Afghanistan. They saw the opportunity to partner with her as
God's answer to their prayer.

Some churches resist the call. One man's church said, "We
only support local missions." Another's objected to a member's
involvement in the Muslim world. One woman's pastor encouraged her to push aside her sense of God's leading and go, instead,
to a place where their church already supported other workers.
A family's church just said, "No. It's too dangerous."

In this, I'm reminded of a disturbing story from Scripture.
The apostle Paul was traveling to Jerusalem. Along the way,
he stayed in Tyre for about a week. The believers he met with
there discouraged him from going on to Jerusalem.[5] We can
only imagine their sorrow and fear as they all knelt down on the
beach, prayed, and said goodbye to one another.[6]

Resolutely, Paul continued his journey, stopping in Ptol-
emais and later Caesarea.[7] In Caesarea, the entire community

"urged him not to go up to Jerusalem."[8] They were sure Paul's call would lead their beloved friend into life-changing danger. Paul cried out, "What are you doing, weeping and breaking my heart?"[9]

I imagine the scene: the believers crying, begging their brother to give up his call and stay safely with them, and Paul, fully human, a man who loved his friends deeply, their cries breaking his heart.

Paul didn't try to convince his brothers and sisters that everything was going to be all right. He didn't speak the often-repeated phrase, "The safest place is in the center of God's will." He didn't rebuke their fears. Instead he said, "For I am ready not only to be imprisoned but even to die in Jerusalem for the name of the Lord Jesus."[10]

Paul's journey to Jerusalem did lead him into bondage and radically changed the course of his life.[11] According to tradition, the apostle Paul was martyred for his faith, but not before he gave us both an example of a believer fully committed to Christ and a collection of treasured letters.[12]

When churches send their children to dangerous places, they enter the Father-heart of God.

God passionately loves the world. God loves the world so much that He sent His Son into the world to touch, heal, teach, save, and die for the world.[13] Jesus Christ, God's Son, came into a very dangerous world,[14] a world full of poverty and violence. He loved deeply the people He encountered.[15] He suffered for having come.[16] He counted the cost, paid the price, and called us worth it.[17]

God calls us fragile, timid, mortal human beings to share His sacrificial and saving love and truth with those who suffer hunger, oppression, and all manner of bondage.

How can we send those we love to dangerous places? We remember that God the Father sent His beloved Son into a terribly dangerous place.

The central story of the gospel is God the Father sending, God the Son going, and God's world needing. When we send our members to dangerous places, we enter the very heart of Father God. We breathe the Spirit of God through our hands and feet and hearts and lips to a world that desperately needs the healing, restoring grace, love, and truth of God.

Some church leaders fully embrace God's heart for the full body of Christ,[18] including those who are born, live, and die in dangerous places. They recognize their role and find joy in equipping of the saints for the work of service,[19] even when that service sends their people far away. They pray for God to call some of their members out into the world. They teach God's love and passion for the world and encourage their members to go. When their members do go, they counsel, pray, celebrate, support, send, and welcome home those who are part of their fellowship. In so doing, they share in God's world-encompassing love.

One pastor writes:

I'm sure all of heaven was tuned into every moment of Jesus' life, waiting, watching, praying, and even at times agonizing. No experience quite mimics this epic story as when we as a body support missionaries who are going into the roughest and most dangerous parts of the world. We see, we watch, we wait, we pray, and we find ourselves living vicariously through the brave souls of our fellow missionaries. —Pierre Eade, pastor, Washington Crossing UMC

Many churches do the hard work of providing opportunities for their members to hear from overseas workers directly. These visits impact the spiritual life of the church and encourage others to go.

I recall meeting a young family that was headed into Iraq. They had been living in relatively safe North Africa when Saddam Hussein was overthrown. They sensed God calling them to take their two small children and move into the heart of a war zone. Their testimony stirred, challenged, and encouraged my own heart as I explored Christ's invitation to walk with Him in Afghanistan.

Most members serving on the field met their first overseas worker at a church gathering. When they did, they felt the Holy Spirit stirring within them, calling them out to the world. For most, the journey took years. The pastor and church leaders who organized that distant gathering may be all but forgotten, but the fruit of their efforts remain.

Overseas workers often took their first trip as part of a small team from their church. There, they saw the needs and opportunities and wondered if God might be calling them to some faraway place.

In a busy church schedule, gatherings featuring overseas workers with their difficult stories and odd clothing can be hard to organize. Short-term trips are expensive in terms of time and energy. And all the while, the day-to-day needs of the church and immediate community demand attention. Yet when churches embrace their role in calling forth, training, and equipping their members to the "good works, which God prepared beforehand, that we should walk in them,"[20] they, too, join the journey. They experience the joys and sorrows of serving God in a dangerous place.

THE DAY-TO-DAY, week-to-week challenges of ministering locally crowd out the voices and faces of those among them who serve in distant lands. The challenge is especially great for those whose members serve in dangerous places. Their pictures and updates can't be posted on the church website. Their stories are often veiled in pseudonyms, and their exact locations hidden.

One pastor writes:

Our church has supported several workers serving God in dangerous places. In every case it gave our own church a greater awareness of what God is doing in the world at large, a deeper sense of participation in the larger cosmic spiritual battle, a greater sympathy and connection with the suffering body of Christ in other

places, and a deeper sense of obligation to pray—all of which I regard as positive signs of spiritual growth and maturity. I know of no better way of weaning us from our tendency to self-absorption and putting our own problems in proper perspective than catching a glimpse of what our brothers and sisters in other places are called upon to endure for Christ's sake. Truly the ways of God, though mysterious, are wise.
—Pastor Keith Harris, Cornerstone Community Church, Hunterdon, NJ

Churches can struggle to stay connected with their members who've left for the field. The day-to-day, week-to-week challenges of ministering locally crowd out the voices and faces of those among them who serve in distant lands. The challenge is especially great for those whose members serve in dangerous places. Their pictures and updates can't be posted on the church website. Their stories are often veiled in pseudonyms, and their exact locations hidden.

Some church leaders find creative ways to embrace the work of those from their church family who invest, on their behalf, in the distant kingdom of God.

One pastor invites a member to read a different email prayer update from their workers each Sunday. By doing so, he invites his community to stay in prayer for God's work in dangerous places. Another pastor includes prayer for his overseas members when he prays from the pulpit each Sunday. My own pastor hosted a telephone call with me during a Sunday morning service. Some pastors actually visit their members on the field. These visits are life-giving to both the members back home and those who labor in oppressive countries.

Often churches struggle to reincorporate their members when they return home to visit or stay. Such members reenter their churches full of stories and passion for a people far away, while their churches are focused on something entirely different.

One church community was in the middle of a capital campaign, raising money to build a new sanctuary, when a member returned with pictures of hungry families in a developing country. Another church was deeply invested in a teaching series the pastor considered critical and viewed their returning overseas worker as a distraction rather than a gift.

Those pastors who embrace their returning members and missionaries the church supports experience benefits that are far greater than the costs incurred.

One pastor writes:

The work which our friend has done for the Lord in distant and dangerous territories has been a tremendous inspiration, example, and challenge not only for the congregation I serve, but also for myself personally. Because of her witness, many within our church community have been encouraged to rise above their fears to serve selflessly and sacrificially. One example of this was the decision of our Kenya missions team to go and

minister in Africa despite the Ebola scare. Our friend powerfully manifests the love, wisdom, and courage of Christ, to whom she's truly and fully given her life.
—Pastor Tim Kriebel, Bethlehem United Methodist Church, Thornton, PA

Those who serve in dangerous places are neither giants nor flawless heroes. Instead, we are our church's living letters,[21] demonstrating the grace, love, and power of God through our willingness to give our lives in service to others. We are part of that "great cloud of witnesses"[22] from Hebrews 11, people who have wandered the face of the earth for our faith.

IN A DIVISIVE SOCIETY, our unity bears witness to the glory of God. We are walking in God's commandment to love one another, declaring by our actions that Christ has, indeed, broken down the dividing walls between us.

Our presence encourages believers to "lay aside every weight, and sin which clings so closely, and let us run with endurance the race that is set before us, looking to Jesus, the founder and perfecter of our faith, who for the joy that was set before him endured the cross, despising the shame, and is seated at the right hand of the throne of God."[23]

When faith communities fully embrace those from their midst who follow Christ into a dangerous land, they share the joys and sorrows of the journey. Through it, they too are changed. Their faith grows deeper and their local and distant ministries grow stronger.

Many of us who go enjoy support from members of diverse churches, small groups, and community ministries. We become the context for shared conversations of faith, hope, and love.

One woman who worked at a Christian bookstore in a small town told me about the many conversations where members of very different local churches shared their latest emails, bits of news, hopes, and prayers for a worker they all supported. In those interactions, the walls of their denominations and churches collapsed and brothers and sisters lived the reality of being one body in Christ, all sharing in His work in the world.

One small group, comprised of members from different churches, began a prayer gathering for someone serving overseas that they shared in common. Their conversation drifted into the frustrations each had in offering Christ's love to those in their lives. Finally, one member reminded the others of their friend overseas. "Look, she can share Christ in that incredibly dangerous place. We ought to be able to do it here, too!" Filled with renewed faith, they found ways to embrace God's call to love even the most difficult people in their lives.

On one trip home from Afghanistan, I hosted a gathering in a public venue for my friends and partners. We realized that members from twenty-two churches gathered in one location to celebrate God's work in a very dangerous place. In our diversity and our faith, we experienced a glimpse of heaven, where people from every tribe nation and tongue gather together to worship the Lord.

I'm reminded of the Scriptures, "We, though many, are one

body in Christ, and individually members one of another."[24] In a divisive society, our unity bears witness to the glory of God. We are walking in God's commandment to love one another, declaring by our actions that Christ has, indeed, broken down the dividing walls between us.[25] "By this all people will know that you are my disciples, if you have love for one another."[26]

The invitation to partner with those who are called to a dangerous place is a privilege that deepens the faith, hope, and love of the churches that embrace it.

Each of us senses the call to open our hands before Christ and, in our doubt and aching inadequacy, ask Him, "But what can I give?" Most of us, before we board the plane, find His guidance for how He wants us to share His love and truth with those who live in the dangerous place to which He's called us. The work we do and the way we do it is as varied as the individuals He calls.

DISCUSSION GUIDE

Chapter 9: How Can We Send Our People?

1. How would you describe the Father-heart of God who sent His Son to a dangerous world?

2. Have members from your own church or faith community left to extend God's love to those far away? What sacrifices and blessings has your community experienced?

3. How does your church encourage members to go?

4. How does your faith community continue to support members while they're working in distant lands?

5. How does your church welcome members when they return home?

6. Brainstorm ways you can encourage and support those you know who are serving in dangerous places.

Chapter 10

WHAT DOES GOD CALL US TO DO?

"Whoever believes in me will also do the works that I do; and greater works than these will he do, because I am going to the Father."
—John 14:12

God wraps His love and truth in our hearts and minds and bodies. He invites us to enter the world with Him, but what does He call us to do?

Are we meant to only build churches, ring bells, and invite people to worship? Are we meant to stand on street corners, sit in cafés, and talk to all who pass by about the saving grace of Jesus Christ? Are we meant to raise money, build orphanages, and care for abandoned children? Or should we plant trees, build roads, provide medical care, teach, or help mend broken relationships?

What does God call us to do?

I wonder if the fishermen, James and John, asked that same question. Did they sit in the back of the crowded synagogue in Nazareth and watch as Jesus, their new teacher, received a hand-written copy of an ancient prophecy? Did they wait silently, expectantly, as Jesus carefully unrolled the scroll? Did they lean forward at the sound of the familiar, beautiful words?

> The Spirit of the Lord is upon me,
> because he has anointed me
> to proclaim good news to the poor.
> He has sent me to proclaim liberty to the captives
> and recovering of sight to the blind,
> to set at liberty those who are oppressed,
> to proclaim the year of the Lord's favor.[1]

Did the fishermen sigh as Jesus "rolled up the scroll and gave it back to the attendant"?[2] Did they notice that everyone in the synagogue was watching their new teacher intently, each wondering what He would say?[3]

Jesus sat down, the center of everyone's attention, "and he began to say to them, 'Today this Scripture has been fulfilled in your hearing.'"[4]

Immediately, an argument arose. Some marveled, others challenged. Jesus engaged. In the end, the Sabbath day worshipers "rose up and drove him out of the town."[5]

James, John, and the others who had begun to follow Jesus continued on their journey with Him. As they traveled, they watched Jesus teach the good news of the kingdom of God, confront and overcome demonic forces, and heal many who were sick.[6]

Did the words Jesus spoke in that Nazareth synagogue echo in their hearts? "The Spirit of the Lord is upon me."[7] Did they watch with wonder as day after day their Master fulfilled those very words? Did they expect Jesus to call them to do the same when He named them apostles?[8] After all, an apostle is one who is sent.

I imagine James and John, standing on the hillside, listening as Jesus taught thousands of people the meaning of the kingdom of God.[9] Then they watched their Master heal a centurion's servant, resurrect a widow's dead son, comfort a group of grieving emissaries, and forgive a woman who had sinned.[10]

Finally, it was their turn to go. "And he [Jesus] called the twelve together and gave them power and authority over all demons and to cure diseases, and he sent them out to proclaim the kingdom of God and to heal."[11] In effect, He said go, help people in their places of greatest need, and tell them about Me.

Jesus' commandment echoes God's words to Abraham when He called him to leave his homeland. "You will be a blessing ... and in you all the families of the earth shall be blessed."[12]

James and John had seen Jesus' example, the ways He taught, healed, comforted, showed mercy, fed hungry people, and more. With all they had witnessed, they and others set off on their first missionary trip. They still had much to learn.

After they returned, Jesus continued to teach and model the

mission He was inviting them to share.

They watched their Master help even more people. They listened to His parables and struggled to understand and apply the full scope of His meanings.

They learned the importance of good works: feeding the hungry, providing water to the thirsty, welcoming the stranger, clothing the naked, and visiting the sick and imprisoned.[13] They also learned that many would believe in Jesus through their words, and those who did so were important to their Master.[14]

After the long and heartbreaking journey to the cross and the cave, they retreated, locking themselves in a room "for fear of the Jews."[15] Perhaps they thought their journey with Jesus was over.

In their grief, confusion, and fear, "Jesus came and stood among them and said to them, 'Peace be with you.' When he had said this, he showed them his hands and his side."[16]

We can only imagine how James, John, and the others felt. Later, John wrote, "Then the disciples were glad when they saw the Lord."[17] They still had much to learn about what it means to follow Christ into the world.

"Jesus said to them again, 'Peace be with you. As the Father has sent me, even so I am sending you.'"[18]

That simple sentence, "As the Father has sent me, even so I am sending you,"[19] contained every aspect of Christ's journey on earth: His vulnerable birth, His simple childhood obedience, His baptism in water and battle with Satan in the wilderness, His teachings, His healings, and even His sufferings. Perhaps James and John recalled the words their Teacher spoke on the night He was betrayed: "Truly, truly, I say to you, whoever believes in me will also do the works that I do; and greater works than these will he do, because I am going to the Father."[20]

In that moment on the hillside, Jesus breathed on His disciples "and said to them, 'Receive the Holy Spirit.'"[21] Ah the Holy Spirit, the Helper Jesus promised, the One who would be forever with them, the One who would teach them all things and bring to their remembrance all that Jesus had said to them.[22] They would continue to learn.

On their last day with Him, "Jesus came and said to them, 'All authority in heaven and on earth has been given to Me. Go therefore and make disciples of all nations, baptizing them in the name of the Father and of the Son and of the Holy Spirit, teaching them to observe all that I have commanded you. And behold, I am with you always, to the end of the age.'"[23]

We know only a little of what happened next. The most authoritative account we have is that which is recorded in the book of Acts. From Acts, we know that Peter preached a powerful sermon;[24] he and John healed a lame man;[25] and James, John's brother, was brutally killed.[26] Even in those short accounts, we see Jesus-followers preaching, healing, and suffering.

Most of the book of Acts, from chapter 9 onward, focuses on the life and ministry of Paul. We read about his conversion, his tireless travels, his fearless preaching, and his wise leadership. Through his epistles, we read more of his journeys and ministry. We know that he made tents, but his primary focus was clearly on teaching the Word and establishing churches.

We know very little of the lives and ministries of most of the apostles, let alone the multitude of unnamed Christ-followers who, empowered by the Holy Spirit, went out to the world.

The apostle Paul, about whom much is written and who wrote much, has come down through history as our model of a missionary: healer, teacher, preacher, and church planter. Yet Paul understood clearly the diversity of the church. "For just as the body is one and has many members, and all the members of the body, though many, are one body, so it is with Christ. For in one Spirit we were all baptized into one body—Jews or Greeks, slaves or free—and all were made to drink of one Spirit."[27]

ONE MAN I KNOW keeps his beard long, sits with Muslim men in teahouses and mosques, and shares the love and truth of Christ. Through his conversations, many have come to know Christ for themselves and have found their lives transformed.

He asks us to consider, "Are all apostles? Are all prophets? Are all teachers? Do all work miracles?"[28] The answer is clearly no. Not everyone will preach, teach, and heal like Paul did. Nor will everyone manage the distribution of resources like Stephen did.[29]

Paul wrote, "Now there are varieties of gifts, but the same Spirit; and there are varieties of service, but the same Lord; and there are varieties of activities, but it is the same God who empowers them all in everyone."[30] Paul urged each of us to "walk in a manner worthy of the calling to which you have been called."[31]

What does God call us to do?

He calls us to love and serve the world with the unique talents, passions, gifts, and abilities that He's given us. Paul made this quite clear.

> Having gifts that differ according to the grace given to
> us, let us use them: if prophecy, in proportion to our
> faith; if service, in our serving; the one who teaches, in
> his teaching; the one who exhorts, in his exhortation;
> the one who contributes, in generosity; the one who
> leads, with zeal; the one who does acts of mercy, with
> cheerfulness.[32]

I've had the privilege of knowing workers gifted in many diverse ways. Each has a name I can't share, but their stories declare the glory of God.

I've known evangelists, teachers, and preachers who have lived and worked in some of the most dangerous places on earth. These are men and women gifted by God to proclaim the kingdom of God, to share the good news of Christ's sacrificial death and resurrection, to call people to repentance, and to nurture, train, and equip believers.

One man I know keeps his beard long, sits with Muslim men in teahouses and mosques, and shares the love and truth of Christ. Through his conversations, many have come to know Christ for themselves and have found their lives transformed.

An older woman visits Muslim women in their homes. She

shares the gospel in stories, pictures, and parables. She prays with women and watches them find salvation and healing.

One young woman speaks only English. She shares the gospel daily with English-speaking college students. Through their conversations, young Muslim men and women meet Jesus, find Him beautiful, and commit their lives to following Him.

These are evangelists, gifts of God for the church without walls, the body of Jesus Christ. They help people "to know and to believe the love that God has for us,"[33] a love so great "that he gave his only Son, that whoever believes in him should not perish but have eternal life."[34]

I've also known pastors and teachers who meet one-on-one or with groups of seekers and believers. One woman and her coworkers gathered women together from surrounding villages in a stiflingly hot, crowded room to teach those gathered the foundations of the saving work of Christ, how to read and apply Scripture, how to pray, and how to live in holiness.

A blond, blue-eyed man met weekly with a group of Muslim-background believers. Behind thick walls and closed doors, the men worshiped, prayed, and studied Scripture.

Another man met regularly with a small group of emerging national pastors, men committed to carrying the gospel of Jesus Christ to their neighbors, extended family members, and even strangers, despite the extreme danger of doing so in the Muslim country they called home.

All these workers labor primarily in word and prayer. Like the apostle Paul, they have been "made minister[s] according to the gift of God's grace, which was given [them] by the working of his power."[35]

Each of these individuals knows the joy and passion of serving as they were created to do. Yet we ought not think of their work as the only, nor even the greatest, model of what God calls us to do in dangerous places. Paul's testimony about himself makes this clear. "Though I am the very least of all the saints, this grace was given, to preach to the Gentiles the unsearchable riches of Christ."[36]

The call to preach, teach, and evangelize is, in and of itself, a grace, a gift of God given to individuals for the sake of Christ and His people. Others carry different gifts into dangerous lands.

A Christian pediatrician trains national doctors, provides consultations for workers scattered across the country, treats sick and injured children, and ministers grace and love to their parents.

A Muslim family brings a son with a significant birth defect to a Christian nurse. She makes arrangements with an aid organization to fly the boy to America, where he receives life-restoring surgery, and she returns him, healed, to his family.

A Muslim woman brings a foreign friend to visit a neighbor. The neighbor's husband is wasting away with tuberculosis. The foreigner, a Christ-follower, connects the man with an NGO that provides vital, life-saving medicines and the food the man needs to recover. Within months, the man, restored to health, returns to work.

Each of these—a doctor, a nurse, and an aid worker—

follow Jesus' example as they heal the sick. They do so as Christ-followers, men and women who love both Jesus and their neighbors. As they minister to those in need, they share the love and truth of God through the unique gifts, talents, and abilities that God has placed in their hands.

One father, a Muslim religious leader, returned with his healed daughter full of gratefulness. He said, "That foreign doctor, he was so kind. Generous. And can you believe he's a Christian?" He held his daughter's hand and repeated, "He was so kind."

Jesus said, "In the same way, let your light shine before others, so that they may see your good works and give glory to your Father who is in heaven."[37]

WHAT DOES GOD call us to do in dangerous places? He calls us to love Him and love our neighbors, even when our neighbors claim to be our enemies.

A family leaves the "safety" of their suburban life, moves into a crime-ridden, inner-city neighborhood and feeds those living on the streets. An elderly woman walks dark city streets looking for hungry, thrown-away children and brings them into a local shelter. These, too, shine their light in dark places.

In the worst Afghan winter on record, my friends and I distributed blankets to the poorest of the poor in our community. Over the course of several frigid days, shivering Afghan boys and girls, young men and women, and a small group of foreign Christ-followers packed handmade blankets into vans, drove over icy roads, pounded on gates, and gleefully delivered our small gifts to those in need.

We didn't stop to preach or hand out tracts. We gave blankets, offered words of blessing, gave thanks to God, and rushed off to the next family. As we gave, we knew the joy of exercising a "religion that is pure and undefiled before God, the Father."[38]

Those who helped distribute those blankets and those who received them knew that the foreigners, the Christ-followers in their midst, had chosen to help them. In doing so, we who shared God's gifts revealed the love of God, a love so extreme, so complete, that it touches all our hearts and draws us toward Him.

Some of us who packed blankets that winter were project managers, others trainers, one an educator. We lived and worked as part of a community of diversely gifted Christ-followers. Our community also included agriculturalists, teachers, wives raising small children in the company of Afghan neighbors, and even accountants. Each of us brought the gifts, talents, and passions Christ gave us and offered them, open-handed, to those in need.

What does God call us to do in dangerous places? He calls us to love Him and love our neighbors, even when our neighbors claim to be our enemies. Jesus said, "But I say to you, Love your enemies and pray for those who persecute you, so that you may be sons of your Father who is in heaven. For he makes his sun rise on the evil and on the good, and sends rain on the just and on the unjust."[39]

One Afghan woman, a trainer with one of my projects, poured me a cup of tea and demanded to know why I had come to her country. I smiled and then told her about Jesus and His love. I told her about those from Europe and the United States who had donated money for our project and offered their prayers for her.

Astonished, she shook her head. "Our Muslim leaders say you are our enemies, but you Christians help us."

Love expressed in word and deed reveals God's love for the world, even for those who don't yet know Him.

God calls some to work toward justice for the oppressed. His people establish shelters for street children, rescue the enslaved from traffickers, and work with local governments to set up court systems capable of providing justice for the most vulnerable. They fulfill God's call "to loose the bonds of wickedness, to undo the straps of the yoke, to let the oppressed go free, and to break every yoke."[40]

God's people also advocate for the rights of workers, women and children, and minority populations. Some seek to change the systemic causes of poverty, prejudice, and enslavement woven into the structures of societies. In doing so, they "open [their] mouth for the mute, for the rights of all who are destitute . . . [and] defend the rights of the poor and needy."[41]

Others carry God's invitation to reconciliation and peace into bitter and violent conflict zones. They encourage warring factions to lay down their arms, share a common meal, and see the humanness in one another. They invite the perpetrators of violence to repentance and the victims of that same violence to forgiveness. These are the peacemakers, the ones whom Jesus said would be called the sons of God.[42]

These, too, are things God calls His people to do in dangerous places.

There are others whose gifts seem so small, yet God calls them precious. A young Christian man works out each week at a local gym. He gets to know some of the other young men and through friendship shares the love and grace of Christ. A mother welcomes a local woman into her home to help her with her house and children. The women become closer than sisters, transforming each other's lives through their companionship. A group of foreign men join a volleyball game and afterward trade stories, laughter, and faith with their new Muslim friends.

Each of us who goes carries the gifts of our unique personality with us. Some are extroverts, others introverts. Some are visionaries and others are highly detailed. Some are deeply relational and others focus on information or tasks.

When a young American woman who visited with me for a summer arrived in Afghanistan, she wondered what she could possibly give. She thought that all workers were extroverted, bold, and highly relational. She couldn't imagine how she could fit. After all, she was an introvert, cautious, and precise and detailed in her work.

At the end of the summer I asked her what she'd learned during her season in Afghanistan. Her simple response both surprised and delighted me. "There's a place for me here."

I thought of a verse from the book of Ephesians: "For we are His workmanship . . ." each with our own unique personality, gifts, and abilities ". . . created in Christ Jesus for good works, which God prepared beforehand, that we should walk in them."[43]

When that young woman joined me for the summer, she taught English to Afghan high school girls. The girls welcomed her not only into their classes, but also into their hearts. Along the way, my young visitor shared God's love and truth with people I would never have met. I celebrated that young woman's journey and remain deeply grateful for the opportunity to watch her give of herself so generously.

Wrapped in the unique gifts, talents, abilities, and personality of each person who goes is the presence of Christ within our very human thoughts, emotions, and bodies.[44] It's His presence that is the hope of glory.[45]

Those who go are the salt of the earth and the light of the world,[46] seasoning and shining in some of the darkest places on earth. They do the good works God has prepared for them to do[47] and in so doing, they each show a fragment of the nature of God who revealed Himself most fully in Christ Jesus.[48]

In lands without church buildings, we raise our voices in worship, extend our hands to bless, and fall to our knees to pray. We are Christ's ambassadors[49] to nations thick with the scent of death. We go so that those whom God loves might experience the fragrance of Christ and find life.[50]

We are not the saviors. We reveal Christ, but the work is always His. We ache to see people come to know Him and grieve when those who do suffer terribly for their faith. This, too, is part of the journey.

DISCUSSION GUIDE

Chapter 10: What Does God Call Us to Do?

1. How do works of service—healing the sick, feeding the hungry, sheltering the homeless—reflect the heart of God?

2. How do preaching, teaching, and evangelism reflect the heart of God?

3. Consider 1 Corinthians 12:12–13. How does the diversity of ministries and ministers communicate God to the world?

4. Read 2 Corinthians 4:7 and write it down. Consider the treasure God has placed within you. What is it like for you to have this treasure?

5. Read a portion of Jesus' prayer in John 17:18–23. Who is Christ calling you to share His love and truth with in this season of your life? Write a prayer for them in your journal.

Chapter 11

IT'S ALL OF HIM

"There is an invitation to humility in walking with Christ in a dangerous place. We are not the saviors. We are flesh and blood human beings called to be His presence, to love people He loves and to share His stories with them."

Shortly after I arrived in Afghanistan, I made friends with the women of an Afghan extended family in my neighborhood. Each week we met together, drank tea, and talked. They taught me how to live in their country, and I introduced them to Jesus.

After six months of sharing tea and conversation, we sat down to watch the *Jesus Film*.[1] They loved the movie and admired the goodness and wisdom they saw in Jesus. When it was over, they fell into conversation. While they talked, I prayed.

Finally, after more than twenty minutes, they gave me their decision; while they really liked Jesus, they would not follow Him. They asked me to continue visiting, but told me they didn't want to hear any more about the Honorable Jesus Messiah.

I was heartbroken.

I walked home that day full of questions: Had I said something wrong, had I failed to pray enough, was there something else I should have said? I replayed every conversation I'd had with that family. I looked for my failures and found them far too easily. By the time I arrived at my house, I was sure that I was at fault. If only my language had been better . . . If only I understood the culture . . . If only . . .

A young student in America asked me what the hardest thing was about living and working on the field. Immediately, a list of challenges scrolled through my mind, but I think this is the hardest: sometimes we give everything we have only to find that it's not enough.

The night my Afghan friends said no, I prayed, and as I did so, I found my rest in Jesus. I remembered that no matter what, He loved those women. And I remembered that His work in them wasn't finished, regardless of their decision that day.

Since that heartbreaking conversation, I've had the privilege of hearing the testimonies of many Afghans who've come to faith. As I shared earlier, virtually all share the same experiences. Each had met a Christ-follower and experienced a fragment of Scripture. Each also experienced a personal revelation, usually through a dream but sometimes in the form of a vision. Each counted the cost, wrestled through the implications, and committed their lives to Christ; and, of course, each had faced persecution. For all, the journey took years.

I knew that my little group of women friends had met a

Christ-follower when they met me. I also knew that they had experienced Scripture both through my stories and the film. However, until the Spirit of God spoke to them directly, they would not put their lives in Christ's hands. The words of Jesus are clear. "No one can come to me unless the Father who sent me draws him."[2]

I knew that God loved each of those women. I knew He loved them more than I ever could. He created each one of them, knitting them together in their mothers' wombs. He was with them when they were born. He heard their first cry and watched them take their first steps. He was with them on their wedding day, and He was with us in that room as they watched the film, considered His Son, and said no. And of course He was still with them long after I had walked away.[3]

I also understood that God was revealing Himself to those precious women, women He had loved from the foundations of the earth, women He had sent His Son to save. He was drawing them to Himself in ways of His choosing, according to His time-frame, and not according to mine.

There is an invitation to humility in walking with Christ in a dangerous place. We are not the saviors. We are flesh-and-blood human beings called to be His presence, to love people He loves, and to share His stories with them. It's God who births faith in people's hearts.[4]

After several years of absence, I returned to the neighbor-hood where those women lived. I had no plans to seek any of them out. However, as is so often the case, God had His own plan.

As I walked down a dusty alley on my way back to my borrowed home, a young teenage girl cried out my name and threw her arms around me. I recognized her as the half-grown daughter of one of the women from the extended family I had met with years earlier.

The girl grabbed both my hands and half dragged me into her family's compound. Moments later, I found myself sitting with her mother, drinking tea, and eating slices of moist cucumber laced in salt. We traded our news, where I'd gone, the work I'd done, and the children she'd married off and birthed. In the course of our conversation, I told her that I had come to town to attend the funeral of an Afghan friend.

The woman's eyes filled with tears. She looked down at the carpeted floor between us and spoke her heart. "I'm afraid of dying. I'm afraid of being put in the ground. I'm afraid of what will happen next."

Her words took my breath away. I prayed and began to share. That day, that dear woman who had said no to Christ some seven years before said yes. I watched her tears vanish into joy and knew that Christ had drawn her to Himself.

How can we keep living, keep loving, and keep giving in the dangerous places God calls us to? We remember, day after day, that Jesus loves us all and His Spirit is working within us and within our neighbors. Sometimes, we have the privilege of seeing the fruit of God's Spirit in our own lives and in the lives of others. When we do, we rejoice. Other times, we walk by faith, confident in the things we hope for, the things we don't yet see.[5]

Often I've recalled Jesus' parables; the kingdom of God is like a mustard seed, small, seemingly irrelevant and nearly invisible, yet it grows.[6] "The kingdom of God is like a man who casts seed upon the soil; and he goes to bed at night and gets up by day, and the seed sprouts and grows—how, he himself does not know."[7] We plant the Word through our presence, words, deeds, and prayers, and God provides the increase.[8] Sometimes we have the privilege to see it; other times we don't.

I'm reminded of a story from the days of the Indo–Pakistani war. The countryside was full of violence. Armed gunmen, intent on destruction, killed indiscriminately. A warrior full of rage and hatred seized an old woman, but she refused to cower in fear. Instead, she rebuked her assailant. She called him to repentance and challenged him to return to the decency for which he was created.

That warrior continued to rob, kill, and destroy, but the words of the old woman haunted him. Eventually, his hatred collapsed. He laid down his arms, cried out for forgiveness, and offered his life to Christ. That man became an evangelist, carrying the good news of the gospel all across Pakistan.[9]

God is orchestrating His work through His people and through His Spirit. The work belongs to Him, and He alone will receive the glory. Our call is to love Jesus and our neighbors well.

In dangerous places, we walk among strangers; some seek to kill us, some welcome us, and many simply watch us.

OUR CALL IS TO SERVE, always aware of God's presence in even the most difficult situations, always hopeful that He is doing a work, even when we can't see it.

Sometimes we can recognize the desires and motivations of those with whom we engage. A worker from the United States told me of a group of young men who approached him on an Afghan street. "We heard you will pay us if we become Christians. We have become Christians. What will you give us?"

Wisely, the man responded. "The payment is suffering. Do you want that?" He went on to sketch the long history of martyrs in the church.

The young men walked away, yet only God knows what that conversation birthed within them.

Another group of young men in a different city approached a foreigner and asked for a copy of the New Testament. The man considered their request and, after much prayer, provided the book. The request had been a trap. The following day, the foreigner was ordered to leave the country. The situation looked like a loss, but again, only God knows what seeds were sown in the hearts of those young men.

Our call is to serve, always aware of God's presence in even the most difficult situations, always hopeful that He is doing a work, even when we can't see it.

The neighborhood elders in one of the communities in which I and a group of coworkers lived demanded that we leave. Within hours, we packed all of our belongings and evacuated our home. The loss left us confused and disoriented.

In the days and weeks that followed, our Afghan neighbors argued among themselves. Those who knew us and had welcomed us were ashamed at what had happened. They saw clearly the integrity of their Christian neighbors and just as clearly the sins of some of their Muslim neighbors. They were shocked and embarrassed at the false accusations breathed against us and the unbridled greed of those who expected payment from us. Their experience demonstrates the truth of Jesus' teaching when He warned us that His presence will bring divisions.[10]

Our part is to love well, walk in integrity, serve wholeheartedly, and trust God, especially for what we cannot see.

In Afghanistan, I learned to hold on to that trust. I learned to remind myself that God loves those young men who were seeking financial gain. He loves the men who asked for a New Testament, even if their actions were intended to trap. He loves our Afghan neighbors, both those who accused and those who defended us. God loves each of them and is doing a work in their lives.

The light shines in the darkness and the darkness reacts. Sometimes the reaction is brutal, violently destroying the lives of people we love. Still we continue, trusting God for what we cannot yet see.

God loves the men who killed and kidnapped our friends and coworkers in Afghanistan, just as He loved the Pakistani warrior confronted by the old woman. He loves them and desires that none should perish, but that all should come to repentance.[11]

We don't pray for the destruction of our enemies, no matter what they do to us and to those we love. Instead, we pray that they would experience God's love and truth. That they would climb out of their physical, mental, and emotional caves, lay down their weapons, and allow themselves to be enveloped by God's holy love.

Indeed, the light shines in the darkness and the darkness reacts, sometimes violently, but still, it's transformed.

I'm reminded of Jesus' entry into our world. Yes, shepherds heard the news and came to worship. Magi saw the star, followed it, and offered their gifts. But not everyone rejoiced. King Herod sent soldiers.[12] "A voice was heard in Ramah, weeping and loud lamentation, Rachel weeping for her children; she refused to be comforted, because they are no more."[13]

An aid worker wrote the following words just days after a dear friend and his children were killed in Afghanistan:

> It is amazing how often in our Christmas advent
> services the readings from Matthew and the killing of
> the innocents are missed out from the happy bleached
> nativity scenes, but the truth is Jesus was born into the
> killing of all of his peers, every boy murdered, every
> family grieving, missing a child; a whole generation
> marked by violence and Jesus fled as a refugee. And it
> is the same today—in Syria, in Iraq, and in so many
> places. —A worker in Afghanistan

What should we say? Jesus, don't come. Don't enter the world; not in Bethlehem, not in Afghanistan or Somalia or Sudan. It's too hard, too painful. The violence is too great.

No, we don't say these things. Instead, we say with the worker quoted above: "His Spirit calls us to go and love and speak of His reconciliation, hope, forgiveness and His abiding with us—in war zones, malls or the quietness of our own hearts."

We go, trusting that God will use us in profound, sometimes visible, but often invisible ways. We enter the traumas of our neighbors, their darkness, and shine the light of the God we know. Along the way, our lives are filled with unexpected blessings and our faith is deepened. One woman writes:

I'VE HAD THE PRIVILEGE of learning two foreign languages in my lifetime, Spanish and Dari. But the words I learned in each are different. I never learned the Spanish words for kidnapping, rape, torture, rockets, or explosions. These I learned in Dari, and I learned them from the women who shared their stories with me.

> What I gained from my time in Afghanistan were kisses from elderly toothless women, who had lived a lifetime by 40; an ability to drink massive amounts of green tea in a single sitting accompanied by the questions, stories, and laughter of women; memories of eating oily eggs with nan (bread) in a house made

of dirt; enough sorrow to overflow the Mississippi as I heard their stories of war and in turn experienced my own losses when people from our aid community were killed, and the realization that when I can find the goodness of God through all the struggles, the laughter, and the tragedy, then I have a faith that is worth sharing. —An aid worker in Afghanistan

I've had the privilege of learning two foreign languages in my lifetime, Spanish and Dari. But the words I learned in each are different. I never learned the Spanish words for kidnapping, rape, torture, rockets, or explosions. These I learned in Dari, and I learned them from the women who shared their stories with me.

IS CHRIST SUFFICIENT? Is He enough? Is He enough for a woman whose husband beats her? Is He enough for a mother who loses her daughter to pay a debt? Is He enough for a man whose legs have been eaten by a mine?

A few months after I arrived in Afghanistan, I stood in a worship service with a small group of other foreigners. That day, we sang about a Christ who quiets our fears, stays firm in chaos, and who is always enough.

That day, I wept as I sang, the stories of too many Afghan women friends crashing in my heart. I asked myself, is Christ sufficient? Is He enough? Is He enough for a woman whose husband beats her? Is He enough for a mother who loses her daughter to pay a debt? Is He enough for a man whose legs have been eaten by a mine?

In America, with my good job, my safe home, and the community of friends and family, I could sing those words without tears. But Afghanistan and every dangerous place in the world is different.

> Historically and globally Christianity has gone through a major shift. One hundred and fifty years ago the majority of Christians were in the rich western/northern world. That is no longer true. The northern/western reality is only 10% of the world church, which means that 90% of Christians are living in possible poverty, violence, and conflict—in the shadow of death. —An aid worker in Afghanistan

When my friends and neighbors in Afghanistan committed their lives to Christ, their problems weren't solved. Women were still beaten. Girls were still sold, and men were still maimed and killed. The same is true in Iraq, Syria, and a dozen other dangerous places in the world. And yet people do give their lives to Christ.

> According to Al-Jazeerah's interview with Sheikh Ahmad Al Katani, the president of The Companions Lighthouse for the Science of Islamic Law in Libya, every hour, 667 Muslims convert to Christianity. Every

day, 16,000 Muslims convert to Christianity. Every
year, 6 million Muslims convert to Christianity.[14]

In this interview, Sheikh Ahmad Al Katani referred to the
conversions of Muslims to Christianity in Africa. Muslims also
embrace Christ throughout the Muslim world. They not only
give their lives to Christ; they suffer intense persecution for
doing so.

Several years ago a young Muslim-background believer
entered his parents' home and declared his faith in Jesus to his
elderly father and two grown brothers. The two brothers beat
him senseless and threw him out on the street. The young man
sought refuge with friends who urged him to flee the country.
He refused.

Several months later, one of the brothers left home to work
in a different part of the country. Shortly after that, the other
brother suffered a serious injury.

The young Christ-follower prayed and returned to his father's house to care for his injured brother. For months, he carried his brother back and forth to the outdoor bathroom. He
bathed his brother, tended to his wounds, and helped him dress.

Initially, the injured brother cursed him constantly. Slowly,
over time, he saw his brother's patient love and accepted his
care. Eventually, his respect and admiration for his brother grew.
When he was finally able to care for himself, he embraced his
brother and welcomed him back into the family.

For this young Christ-follower, Jesus was enough. He experienced the truth of this promise. "If you are insulted for the name of Christ, you are blessed, because the Spirit of glory and of God rests upon you."[15]

Jesus said, "I am with you always, even to the end of the age"[16] and "In the world you will have tribulation. But take heart; I have overcome the world."[17]

When we receive Christ, we receive the Holy Spirit of the living God. We are made alive in Christ. We become God's sons and daughters.[18] We are born again to a living hope.[19] Christ lives within us. Afghan, Syrian, Kurd, American, we live by trusting in the Son of God, who loves us completely and who gave Himself for us.[20]

Christ-followers in dangerous places suffer. In their suffering, they prove, just as the early Christians did, that Christ is sufficient.

A young Muslim woman gave her life to Christ then returned to her family to announce her newfound faith. Her father, a military man, beat her mercilessly. The woman fled.

As soon as her wounds healed, she returned to her father's home. Again, he beat her savagely. When those wounds healed, she returned again, only to face the same violent response.

For several years, she continued to return to her father. The beatings were horrific, emotionally and physically, but she wouldn't give up. Christ had called her to love her father and so she did, trusting God to move in his heart.

Finally, her father beat her for the last time. In the midst of his violence, the young woman cried out, "Father. Father. I am your daughter. Love me!"

The man collapsed, sobbing. He begged his daughter's forgiveness and welcomed her back into his heart and his home.

We who sojourn with men and women of such great faith are encouraged and strengthened. We see the power and sufficiency of Christ in astonishing ways.

In the most dangerous places, faith doesn't look like bumper stickers and T-shirts. It doesn't even look like Sunday morning church services or midweek Bible studies. Instead, it looks like a gray-bearded man memorizing Scripture, then burning the pages lest they be found. It looks like a woman choosing to live in peace with her husband's second wife. It looks like a mother accepting and loving an unwanted daughter-in-law. It looks like a group of women gathering to pray and share stories. It looks like an old woman dying, knowing where she's going.

When we love vulnerable human beings and see their struggles and persecutions, we must hold on to this: Christ is enough, for them and for us.

DISCUSSION GUIDE

Chapter 11: It's All of Him

1. Consider John 6:44. How did God call you or draw you to Himself?

2. Write out Ephesians 2:8. What does it mean to you that you have been saved by grace and not by works?

3. Read John 17:18–23. With whom is God calling you to share His love and truth in this season of your life? Pray for them right now.

4. Consider Mark 4:26–29. What is your part in sharing God's love and truth, and what is God's part in bringing someone to salvation?

5. Have you ever watched someone you love reject Christ? What was that like for you?

Chapter 12

KNOWING CHRIST WITH US

"It was like living in the book of Acts as we journeyed with local believers taking risks for the truth and people literally laying down their lives for the sake of the Gospel." —A mother serving in Afghanistan

Jesus never said it would be easy. Quite the opposite. "In the world you will have tribulation."[1] And in truth, I've tasted trouble and suffering—my own and that of others around me. I would have collapsed beneath the weight had Christ not accompanied me. And here, His promise is sure. "I am with you always, to the end of the age."[2]

I imagine John and his brother James standing on the mountainside, listening to Jesus speak those words.[3] How beautiful they must have sounded to the two fishermen. The Jesus they loved would always be with them!

Luke picks up the story. "Then he [Jesus] led them out as far as Bethany, and lifting up his hands he blessed them."[4] I imagine James and John, so full of joy in the presence of their beloved

Jesus. Of course, Jesus was resurrected; He would be with them forever. They must've rejoiced. But Luke continues his account. "While he [Jesus] blessed them, he parted from them and was carried up into heaven."[5]

I've often tried to explain to my Afghan friends that I wasn't alone in their country, but rather that Jesus was with me. Each one wondered what I could mean. Where was He? Clearly not sitting on the cotton floor mat beside me.

John, the follower of Jesus, must have known we would struggle to understand and explain the presence of Christ with us. Inspired by the Holy Spirit, he recorded the promise Jesus gave us during that last evening before His crucifixion. "I will not leave you as orphans."[6] Instead, "He [the Spirit of truth] dwells with you and will be in you."[7]

> **THE SPIRIT OF GOD** works first within us; within the messy, conflicted, proud, frightened, selfish, fallen humanness of our own souls. As we walk, stumble, dance, cry, and laugh with Christ, we are "strengthened with power through His Spirit in our inner beings."

After James, John, and the others watched Jesus depart from them, "they worshiped him and returned to Jerusalem with great joy."[8] Although Jesus had disappeared from before their eyes, they knew they weren't orphans, abandoned to the world. Instead, they carried within them the very presence of God.

We go out to the world with the Spirit of truth, the Paraklētos, within us—the Comforter, Helper, and Counselor. Although we are mere mortals, utterly human, both flawed and graced, we carry within us the treasure of the knowledge of the glory of God.[9] Our very human frame is His temple, a building where the Holy Spirit of the living God dwells.[10]

Like James and John, we go "clothed with power from on high."[11] The power we carry brings forth the fruit of the Spirit within us first, and then, through us to others: "love, joy, peace, patience, kindness, goodness, faithfulness, gentleness [and] self-control."[12]

Werner Groenewald, who was killed in Kabul with his two children, understood the work of the Spirit within him.

Living in submission to God in a dangerous setting made me understand more about depending on God for my well-being. It helped me to fully surrender and let God be my Provider of safety and all other daily needs while He is busy with a great work firstly within me and then through me to the outside world.

The Spirit of God works first within us; within the messy, conflicted, proud, frightened, selfish, fallen humanness of our own souls. As we walk, stumble, dance, cry, and laugh with Christ, we are "strengthened with power through his Spirit in [our] inner being[s]."[13] We are "rooted and grounded in love"[14] and "filled with all the fullness of God."[15]

It's astonishing to me that we who go are the greatest beneficiaries of the gifts God is sharing through us. One woman who
moved with her husband and children into an inner-city US
community told her experience:

> Of course! I thought of the first time I felt bitter look-
> ing out the window of our dilapidated house to the
> prostitute sitting across the street with a needle stick-
> ing out of her arm! Instead of feeling mercy, compas-
> sion, or love I felt anger and fear. I asked God why He
> sent me here, and He gently pointed out my pride.
> After all I did for Him moving here, selling everything,
> leaving family, He had the audacity to call me prideful!
> At that moment I realized that was exactly what it was.
> It was fine for all these people to live in this dangerous,
> drug-infested place, but not *me*. It was the beginning
> of my healing because I found His heart here and my
> freedom! —A wife and mother living in a dangerous
> place in America

In Christ, we open our hands to the world and share the
love, mercy, truth, and grace that we ourselves are receiving
from the God who loves us with an everlasting love. Yes, the call
to a dangerous place is full of sacrifice, but it's also full of blessings. We who go count ourselves privileged. One former worker
writes:

Imagine holding up a diamond. Each way you turn it
gives a different view, but still gorgeous. Like the turn
of the diamond, living in a land like Afghanistan, I was
able to have a glimpse of several facets of Jesus that
I may not have otherwise experienced. His beauty
stands out in a stark land. Living for Jesus among
Afghans was a precious treasure . . . my life was deeply
transformed in that land and transforms the way I live
today, the passions He has called me to. Most importantly, He has given me a deeper love for Him! —MW

Before I went to Afghanistan, I knew Jesus was beautiful.
But my own journey in that country purified my faith and deepened my understanding and experience of Christ. I am today
more in love with Jesus than I've ever been before. Through so
many painful encounters with evil and loss, endless conversations of faith with those from another culture, and the disap-
pointments of my own failures, I've experienced Christ's love,
joy, and peace. I've found Him faithfully shaping, forming, free-
ing, and loving me in ways I could not have imagined before I
followed Him to a dangerous place. Every aspect of my life has
been transformed.

One young man wrote about the impact on his life:

Serving God in a dangerous and challenging place
like Afghanistan helped me to keep my eyes on the
treasures in heaven instead of my own comfortable

Western life in this temporary place called earth. That
focus on God and eternity still helps me to make the
"right" decisions about work, finances, time, and much
more. —A former worker

When we go to a dangerous place, we give up the comforts,
affluence, and relative safety of our lives at home. We lose our
treasured supports; the presence of families, friends, and church
communities; our clothing, language, and lifestyles; access
to privacy and rest. The sacrifices are real. The losses leave us
disoriented and grieving. Yet in our losses, weaknesses, and extreme vulnerability, we lean into Christ and know Him in ways
we couldn't have if we had held on to all our small securities.

When I first moved to Afghanistan, I found the challenges
of day-to-day life exhausting. Many inconveniences I dealt with
well. Bucket baths and the eastern toilet in my home never
bothered me, but the printer could make me crazy. When the
electricity fluctuated—which it often did despite my voltage
regulator—the printer just gave up, usually in mid-print. I don't
know why that, of all things, bothered me so much, but it did.

Such small inconveniences shattered my patience and
soured my humor. I saw the effects in my short responses to
Afghans and foreigners. Yet even these small things drove me
toward Christ. I knew I needed His presence to live in His peace.

Each morning, I made sure to spend at least an hour in
prayer and worship. I learned to practice the daily discipline of
thanksgiving, noticing God's small blessings and thanking Him

for showing me His presence. In a place where I couldn't avoid the people who bothered me, I learned to practice daily repentance and forgiveness. In the absence of my home church and the wonderful, out-loud worship I had so enjoyed, I developed the habit of singing alone to the God I loved. Those times of worship and prayer are sacred memories that I will always treasure.

I recall one Christmas in particular. I had moved to a remote community in Afghanistan and was completely alone and unbearably cold when Christmas morning arrived. I wrapped myself in blankets, stood in my room, and sang the Christmas songs in my hymnal. I interlaced the songs with readings from the Scriptures and enjoyed my own "Lessons and Carols"[16] service. I remembered that all over the world, others were worshiping God in the same ways I was. That morning, that Christmas, I celebrated the joy of Christ's coming with the communion of saints and knew I wasn't alone.

Some Christ-followers move to dangerous countries with their babies and children. They experience both the joys and challenges of raising children in a difficult environment. The cost to such parents is great, but so are the blessings. I've not met any who regretted the journey.

One family from Germany made arrangements for German teachers to come and help educate their children. Over the course of their years in Afghanistan, several young teachers answered the call. Those teachers are still a part of that family. Another couple combined homeschooling with the lessons taught at the local Afghan school. They rejoiced to see their children develop friendships with Afghan children. Yet another group of families combined their efforts to educate the foreign community's children and enjoyed the fellowship of a shared effort. Each recognized Christ's presence with their family as they lived on the field.

OFTEN, WHEN PARENTS sense Christ's call to a dangerous land, they experience fear, but as they respond to the call, they find joy and deep gratefulness.

I've spent hours in Afghan homes in the company of other foreigners and their children. We drank tea and shared stories as blond-haired, blue-eyed boys and girls played happily with brown-haired, brown-eyed Afghan children. I've watched Afghans care for foreigners' children and love them deeply. One day, I watched an Afghan man hold a shovel while a three-year-old blond boy pushed it into the ground. It was such a beautiful sight! The boy walked away two inches taller, and the Afghan man beamed his delight.

Some families faced difficult medical challenges with their children in locations where Western medical care was unavailable. One mother evacuated to Europe when her daughter developed a life-threatening respiratory infection. The father and their other children remained in Afghanistan. After several weeks, the child's health improved, and mother and child returned to Afghanistan.

A family from Ireland serving in a dangerous location wasn't so fortunate. Their young son pulled a pot of boiling oil from an open burner and burned his own small body severely. That

family buried their son in Ireland and returned to their dangerous location, still grieving his loss, and still committed to walking with Christ in the land to which He'd called them. They
knew Christ was with them, even in their loss.

Often, when parents sense Christ's call to a dangerous land,
they experience fear, but as they respond to the call, they find
joy and deep gratefulness. One mother writes:

> The journey to Afghanistan after 9/11 started out with
> facing our giants. I was three months pregnant when
> we felt led to go. Would I trust God with my little one's
> life and ours? Like the Israelites we had a choice, and
> I'm so glad God won over my fears and we did not
> miss out on all the blessings. Three kids later, it was
> an absolute privilege to raise our kids in such a place
> where they saw faith in action. It was like living in
> the book of Acts as we journeyed with local believers
> taking risks for the truth, and people literally laying
> down their lives for the sake of the Gospel. That is now
> a part of my children's spiritual legacy. They experi-
> enced first-hand the cost, the risk, and the worth of the
> message. —A mother of three in Afghanistan

Each of the parents I've spoken with tells a similar story. They
recognize that the journey has enriched their lives and the lives
of their children. They see the blessings they and their children

experience in walking with Christ in a dangerous place and count themselves privileged.

We who go know the sweetness and purity of Christ in our weakness, loss, and vulnerability. We recognize that whatever happens to us, He is with us.

Those of us who live with Jesus in a dangerous place often face threats to our lives. We are well aware that we live among people who desire to hurt us and those we love. We experience deep fear and lean into Christ for our comfort, encouragement, and sustenance.

One young mother writes:

I struggled with fear for so long. When God was calling me to a dangerous place, safety was never part of the deal. I think back at all the tears and prayers I prayed that God would protect my loved ones as we served in a difficult, violent place. Looking back, I don't think I ever lived a more full life. I now have a perspective that I would never trade. It was full of pain and grief for friends who gave their lives; never was it easy, but I surprise myself in realizing that I envy those that are with the Father now. They gave and gained everything. There is no other place I would rather be. Close your eyes and jump into the abyss. God will be there . . . and will change you in ways you can only imagine: Beauty from ashes. —A wife, mother, and aid worker

During my last weeks in Afghanistan, I faced the abyss head on. I had just welcomed a group of new workers and was facilitating their in-country training. Less than a week after they arrived, I received a terrifying phone call; an Afghan policeman had detained several members of my team and wanted to take them into custody. They needed help, and they needed it immediately.

Trembling with adrenaline, I threw on my scarf and long coat and rushed to their location. I found them and the Afghan policeman who held them. I had no idea what would happen, but I knew I couldn't let the man take our new workers.

I presented our documents and explained that these people were my guests and that I was responsible for them. As soon as the policeman had recorded our information, I told my team and their very young Afghan helper to return to our temporary home. The policeman followed us. When we reached our gate, I sent the team inside, and stayed outside on the dusty street. I didn't dare retreat behind our walls. I knew that if I did, that Afghan policeman would return with others. They would enter our home, search it, and take us all.

I stood alone on the street before a man intent on doing us harm and negotiated with a wisdom and skill I had never before possessed. I knew the Spirit of God was with me, strengthening and guiding me.

The policeman demanded my team members, insisting on arresting them. When I refused, he demanded the young Afghan helper. Again I refused.

Finally, in a fit of frustration, the policeman yelled at me,

"Missus, I am a policeman. I will arrest someone today!"

The ramification of his words swirled around me. I knew that if he took my new team members, they would be traumatized. They had no language and no experience. I couldn't let them be taken.

I also knew that our Afghan helper was a fatherless young man trying to help his mother. He had been afraid of us and was just gaining confidence in the foreigners who had hired him. I couldn't allow him to be taken either.

If that policeman was going to take anyone, it would have to be me. Yet I knew that if he did, things would not go well for me. I'd heard far too many stories of what some Afghan police do to lone women in their custody. I understood the danger all too clearly.

In those moments I stood on the edge of an abyss, yet even as the darkness rolled toward me, I felt a calm strength rise up within me. I knew Christ was with me.

I thought, *So this is how it happens. This is how my life is torn to shreds,* yet I felt no panic. No fear. Only a calm, steady awareness that no matter what happened to me, Christ would still be with me and He would always love me. Nothing the police could do to me would shame me in Jesus' eyes.

I looked straight at the policeman and heard my own voice, "Then you'll have to take me."

He hesitated and my heart felt quiet, whole, and safe. A verse rose up within me. "Greater love has no one than this: to lay down one's life for one's friends."[17] And I felt God smile. That smile, that sense of "well done, good and faithful servant"[18] filled my heart with peace.

When I offered myself in place of my team and our young Afghan helper, I released my hold on life and experienced a pure, holy oneness with Christ. "Whoever loses their life for me will find it."[19] And I did.

I had stepped into the abyss and found freedom, wholeness, and life.

After a long pause, the policeman threw his hands in the air. "I'm not taking you!"

I was relieved. Still, he wouldn't let me leave.

Over the course of the next hour, I stayed out on the dusty street as men gathered around me: more police, secret police, neighborhood elders, and bearded neighbors. Men argued, debated, watched, and waited.

I stood quietly in the midst of the chaos, aware of the dangers, yet confident in the presence of Christ.

Finally, a senior policeman arrived. He questioned me closely, demanded my documents, and berated me. Men pressed in around me, but still I felt Christ with me. I had no idea if Jesus would deliver me, but I knew I was standing in the gentle power of the Holy Spirit.

When the senior policeman finished yelling at me, he simply sent me away.

I was shocked and elated. I had stood in the sandals of Jesus. I had given my life for my friends. I had known God's smile, and I had been delivered.

Many of us initially follow Christ to dangerous lands full of zeal, convinced of our own strength, commitment, and ideals. We know, cognitively, theologically, that Christ is with us. Along the way, we lose our earthly foundations. We experience failure, loss, and suffering. We come to the end of ourselves and find that Christ is still with us.

We learn to walk with Jesus in humility, limping, as it were, trusting His presence to accompany and guide us. We learn that Christ alone is sufficient and our souls rest in His light[20] even while the darkness swirls around us. Through the experience, we come to Him more deeply and know Him more fully than we ever could have if we had stayed in our safe homelands.

We go ready to serve, to love others with Christ's love, and find ourselves falling deeper in love with Jesus. We experience in the core of our beings the astonishing "love the Father has given to us, that we should be called children of God; and so we are."[21]

We stumble, face giants, and learn, sometimes through harrowing situations, to trust Christ's promise to stay with us.[22] We experience the reality that "neither death nor life, nor angels nor rulers, nor things present nor things to come, nor powers, nor height nor depth, nor anything else in all creation, will be able to separate us from the love of God in Christ Jesus our Lord."[23]

With trembling voices and strong voices, with tears and laughter, in strength and weakness, we know that no matter what happens to us, "We are more than conquerors through him who loved us."[24]

Those fleeting things that once caught our attention and informed our desires fall away. We are stripped of soul-deadening diversions and faith-dulling self-sufficiency. In truth, we lose our lives for Jesus and find our lives in Him. We walk in suffering and recognize the goodness and beauty of God. We are like those who thirsted in the desert and have tasted the sweetest water. We are blessed.

How can we live in a dangerous place? How can we bring our children into such darkness? We can and do, because we know that Christ is with us.

DISCUSSION GUIDE

Chapter 12: Knowing Christ with Us

1. How do you describe Christ's presence with you?

2. Consider John 14:16–17. How do you understand the Holy Spirit's presence within you?

3. Read Galatians 5:22–23. How have you experienced the fruit of the Spirit in your life? Which one means the most to you right now in your journey?

4. Consider Romans 8:38–39. Write these verses down and say them out loud. What are some of the experiences in this world that push us away from God? How do the promises in these verses keep you close to Him in the midst of the hardships of this life?

5. How have you experienced God's love, presence, or blessings in the midst of a difficult season in your life? What was that like for you? Journal a prayer of thanks to Him for meeting you in that season.

Final Thoughts

DEEPLY GRATEFUL

In the early days of the modern missions movement, workers went out with their coffins, expecting never to return. Generations later, workers went to the field expecting to live their entire lives in one location. They planted gardens, raised children, and built lifelong relationships with their neighbors.

Today, a new generation of Christ-followers experiences a new set of challenges. Even as I write this chapter, friends are evacuating their foreign homes and returning to the lands of their birth. Others are exploring new fields and discerning Christ's call to walk with Him in yet another country or community. Many are filling out forms, praying, and hoping for the restoration of visas they've lost along the way.

Each one of us—each of us who has lost our adopted home in the dangerous place God called us to—looks over our shoulders, takes stock, and reflects on the call. One man, a husband and father, shared his reflection in the following words:

Firstly, I have no regrets about serving in a dangerous place—Afghanistan; I don't regret that my wife and I both went there and took our one-year-old son with us. Ironically, I suppose in some ways, I'm actually in a higher-risk category now, driving 30 miles each way to and from work on my motorcycle, than I was then. But that being beside the point . . .

Afghanistan has left an indelible mark on me and in my heart. Serving together with people from wildly different walks of life, nationalities, denominational backgrounds, and just about every other thing you can think of—but all with a love of Jesus and the desire to see His name made known in a place where it was not officially welcomed . . . that's a bond that makes all the other differences pale in comparison.

And then it was gone. The unexpected happened; plans changed. People were killed and friends lost. Time and again.

It is not the easy walk to which we're called. In fact, I suppose if I could make a one-word summation, it would be "loss." We've lost friends and acquaintances. We've lost our identities, lost our place of confidence, and become like babies in a culture and language we struggled to learn. We lost things that we may never get back.

And yet . . . like a proverb from the land to which we went says, "Joy and sorrow are sisters . . ." We may have had deep and profound sorrow, but also profound richness and gain. I will never forget the fellowship. I will never forget the sights and sounds and smells. The quirks of another culture, and the hilarious translations that one oftentimes would see . . . The sense of living life to the fullest, of seeing and feeling like I'd never before: so raw, so real, so . . . unsanitized.

Conventional wisdom would dictate that I shouldn't have been there. Explaining things to some people, even some family members, left them with no more understanding than before. There were many times when I myself felt that I really didn't belong in that confusing and dangerous place. And yet, paradoxically, the deepest and most profound sense that, in fact, I did. —A husband and father from Afghanistan

This young man, his wife and child returned to the home of their birth to deliver another baby. They left their Afghan home with all their possessions and their foreign and Afghan friends, expecting to return in a few months. Instead, the doors slammed shut and they found themselves rebuilding a life they didn't expect to live.

Like this family, I, too, returned to my homeland. I de-boarded a plane, disoriented and mapless, but confident that Christ was still with me. When I returned, friends and family celebrated while I grieved. Well-meaning brothers and sisters in Christ asked me questions for which I had no answers. The journey with Jesus is one of day-to-day obedience walked out with sensitivity to His Spirit.

I am finding my way.

Yet, even as I do, I remain deeply grateful for the years I walked with Jesus in Afghanistan. I have seen Christ and fallen more deeply in love with Him. I have seen people He has loved from the foundations of the earth and have fallen in love with them, as well. Today, I look out the window of my American home and consider myself one of the most blessed of people. God has taken me not only to Afghanistan, but also deep into His heart.

I'm also aware that I carry my own share of grief and post-traumatic stress. Precious friends have been kidnapped. Others have been brutally murdered. I have evacuated under threat of kidnapping, traveled through territories thick with men intent on violence, and faced body-destroying danger.

Afghanistan will always be a part of my life—both the suffering and the joy.

If we are honest, every one of us who has gone and every one of us who has loved someone who has gone has asked the question: Why does God call His children to dangerous places? It's a fair question and we are not the first to ask it.

I take comfort in that recognition and courage to offer the answers I've found.

I also take comfort in the fact that my Jesus, the great God-man, fell on His face and prayed so fiercely that He sweated blood.[1] He stood before the tomb of a beloved friend and wept.[2]

He looked over a city and ached for a lost people.[3]

"A servant is not greater than his master."[4] We are not fearless Navy SEALs, spiritual giants, or sinless saints. We are simply followers of the Jesus we love.

My journey in Afghanistan, like the journeys of so many others in dangerous places, has taken me deep into the heart of God. There, I found both sorrow and joy. No, it was not what I expected. Like the fishermen, James and John, I followed Jesus with a vision and a dream and found a love unlike any I'd ever known.

I have lost my life and found it in Him. In many ways, I've experienced something of the breadth and length and height and depth of God's astonishing love for me, even as I've seen His love for others.

And I'm not finished. Or perhaps it's better to say that God is not finished with me. I'm confident that I will continue to explore the contours of God's love for the rest of my life and throughout eternity.

Yes, I ache for the day when we are all reunited—Afghan, Dutch, English, Australian, German, American, and so many others—rejoicing in the most glorious, most perfect heavenly celebration. I long to look into the face of the Father who loves us so much and who has given so much to bring His precious children home.

And still, I live here, on the earth side of glory, confident that Christ is with me, breath by breath, welcoming me into both His sorrow and His joy.

In April 2014, I received yet another heartbreaking phone call. Another dear friend had been killed, along with two other men, in Kabul, Afghanistan. Immediately, everything within me rebelled. Enough! Enough! I can't take any more loss!

Late in the afternoon, after hours of trembling phone and video calls, I took a long walk, alone with my Jesus. I poured out all my losses, the people I'd loved who had suffered and died, and the ones I'd left behind, alive. When my words were finally spoken, I sensed a gentle question. "Do you wish you'd never gone? Do you wish you'd never loved? Do you wish you'd never known such people?"

I wept.

No. A thousand times, no!

I have walked with people, mere mortals, who have the Spirit of God wrapped in their human flesh; men and women who stepped into the abyss with Jesus, who gave their hands to be His hands, who loved those whom He loves, and who gave their lives for His sake. I would not erase even one such person from my life.

I have gone to a dangerous place with Jesus and I am grateful for the journey. I have and still do love others who are, even now, walking with Jesus in dangerous places and I am grateful for each of them.

God invites all of us to share in the "power of His resurrection and the fellowship of His sufferings."[6] This is the heart of God, a heart that transcends geography and passports; a heart that loves each fragile human being who walks the face of His earth. Our journeys are always first about the heart of God, His heart for us and His heart for others.

When we enter God's heart, we experience His love and receive His invitation to share His love with others. We pray, we give, and we go, because we know God and what He's done for us. We are embraced by Him and embrace His heart for others, too.

God's heart is both our destination and our only real home. Perhaps that's the greatest reason why He calls us to dangerous places, so that we will know His astonishing, sacrificial, life-restoring love.

NOTES

Chapter 1: The Question

1. http://en.wikipedia.org/wiki/Pamir_Airways_Flight_112
2. A mullah is an Afghan religious leader.
3. http://www.nytimes.com/2010/08/08/world/asia/08afghan.html?_r=0

Chapter 2: My Story

1. Jason Elliot, *An Unexpected Light: Travels in Afghanistan* (New York: Picador, 1999).
2. Mark 1:19–20
3. This call to "follow Me" was made to Peter in Matthew 4:19, and the call extended in vv. 21–22 to James and John.
4. Matthew 4:22
5. John 1:14
6. 1 John 3:1
7. John 17:3
8. Matthew 20:20–24
9. Matthew 27:56
10. Mark 16:1–6

Chapter 3: How Deep the Father's Love

1. John 7:37
2. Luke 19:41–44
3. John 11:35
4. Matthew 11:28
5. Psalm 139:2–3
6. Psalm 139:11–12
7. Psalm 139:13
8. Hosea 11:4
9. Hosea 11:3
10. Jeremiah 31:3
11. Isaiah 30:18
12. 2 Peter 3:9
13. Psalm 107:10–14
14. Micah 7:19
15. Psalm 103:2–4
16. John 3:16
17. Psalm 46:9
18. Isaiah 2:4
19. Ibid.
20. Revelation 22:1–2
21. Isaiah 11:6

Chapter 4: God Came First

1. Matthew 4:21
2. Matthew 4:22
3. Matthew 11:29
4. Matthew 16:24
5. Luke 10:1
6. Luke 10:3
7. John 1:29
8. Luke 10:17
9. Pseudonym
10. Luke 8:43–48
11. Luke 10:20

12. John 16:33
13. Matthew 10:17–18
14. Matthew 24:9
15. John 11:8
16. Matthew 16:21
17. John 11:6
18. John 11:7
19. John 11:16
20. Matthew 26:36–46
21. John 10:10
22. Ibid.
23. John 16:33
24. Matthew 28:20
25. Luke 10:3

Chapter 5: God Wants to Fill His Table

1. Revelation 19:6
2. Revelation 7:9
3. Revelation 19:9
4. Matthew 22:4
5. Matthew 22:7
6. Luke 14:21
7. Luke 14:23
8. John 14:2–3
9. 2 Peter 3:9
10. Luke 14:16–23
11. Matthew 22:6
12. Matthew 22:11
13. Revelation 7:9
14. Revelation 19:8
15. Revelation 19:6–8
16. Revelation 22:4–5

17. Revelation 19
18. Revelation 22:2
19. Revelation 21:4
20. John 2
21. 1 Corinthians 15:44
22. 1 Corinthians 15:49
23. John 20:19–20; 21:1, 4
24. 1 Thessalonians 2:19
25. Note: all Afghan names are changed to protect their identities.
26. All Afghan names are pseudonyms.
27. Genesis 3
28. Luke 13:34
29. Luke 15:3–7
30. Luke 15:20

Chapter 6: They Have to Hear, See, Touch

1. 2 Corinthians 4:7
2. "Christ Has No Body," Teresa of Avila (1515–1582)
3. Matthew 13:31–32
4. Matthew 3:17
5. 1 Corinthians 15:6
6. John 20:19
7. John 20:5
8. John 20:9
9. John 20:19
10. John 20:21–22
11. John 1:14
12. Matthew 1:23
13. 2 Corinthians 5:20
14. Matthew 28:20

15. Colossians 1:27

16. 2 Corinthians 5:20

17. Romans 10:14 NLT

18. Matthew 28:19

19. 2 Corinthians 2:15

20. Acts 1:8

21. Luke 9:51–56

22. 1 Peter 3:14–15

23. Matthew 10:14

24. Luke 9:53–55

25. Luke 9:56

26. An Afghan worship song

Chapter 7: Following His Call

1. Name used at the contributor's request.

2. Romans 12:1

3. Romans 12:1

4. This advice came from Tom Little, a man who was killed in Afghanistan.

5. Philippians 1:20–24

6. James 1:17

7. Jeremiah 29:11

8. Romans 8:28 NASB

9. Acts 16:6

10. Acts 16:7

11. Acts 16:10

12. Matthew 4:21–22

13. Mark 10:35–45

Chapter 8: Sending Our Friends and Families

1. To protect the privacy of family members, names of quote contributors are left off.

2. Martin Bell, "The Secret of the Stars," *The Way of the Wolf: The Gospel in New Images* (New York: Ballantine Books 1983 reissue).

3. Luke 2:22–24

4. Luke 2:28–32

5. Luke 2:34–35

6. Luke 2:19

7. Bell, "Way of the Wolf."

8. Lamentations 3:22–23

9. Acts 20:35 NASB

10. Philippians 1:3–5

Chapter 9: How Can We Send Our People?

1. Ephesians 4:5–6

2. Ephesians 4:7–8

3. Luke 21:13

4. "American Christians spend 95% of offerings on home-based ministry, 4.5% on cross-cultural efforts in already reached people groups, and .5% to reach the unreached." (The Traveling Team) http://www.aboutmissions.org/statistics.html/

5. Acts 21:3–4

6. Acts 21:5

7. Acts 21:7–8

8. Acts 21:12

9. Acts 21:13

10. Ibid.

11. Acts 21 and following

12. Pauline epistles

13. John 3:16; Luke 1:26–35; Matthew 1:18–23

14. Luke 2:7; Matthew 2:13–18

15. Matthew 9:36–37; John 13:1

16. John 19:1–18

17. Hebrews 12:2

18. Ephesians 4:1

19. Ephesians 4:12

20. Ephesians 2:10

21. 2 Corinthians 3:1–3

22. Hebrews 12:1 NIV

23. Hebrews 12:1–2

24. Romans 12:5

25. Ephesians 2:14

26. John 13:35

Chapter 10: What Does God Call Us to Do?

1. Luke 4:18–19

2. Luke 4:20

3. Ibid.

4. Luke 4:21

5. Luke 4:29

6. Luke 4:31–42

7. Luke 4:18

8. Luke 6:12–16

9. Luke 6:17–49

10. Luke 7

11. Luke 9:1–2

12. Genesis 12:2–3

13. Matthew 25:31–46

14. John 17:18–23

15. John 20:19

16. John 20:19–20

17. John 20:20

18. John 20:21

19. Ibid.

20. John 14:12

21. John 20:22

22. John 14:26

23. Matthew 28:18–20

24. Acts 2:14–41

25. Acts 3:1–10

26. Acts 12:1–2

27. 1 Corinthians 12:12–13

28. 1 Corinthians 12:29

29. Acts 6:1–6

30. 1 Corinthians 12:4–6

31. Ephesians 4:1

32. Romans 12:6–8

33. 1 John 4:16

34. John 3:16

35. Ephesians 3:7

36. Ephesians 3:8

37. Matthew 5:16

38. James 1:27

39. Matthew 5:44–45

40. Isaiah 58:6

41. Proverbs 31:8–9

42. Matthew 5:9

43. Ephesians 2:10

44. 2 Corinthians 4:7

45. Colossians 1:27

46. Matthew 5:13–14

47. Ephesians 2:10

48. Hebrews 1:3

49. 2 Corinthians 5:20

50. 2 Corinthians 2:15–16

Chapter 11: It's All of Him

1. http://www.jesusfilm.org/
2. John 6:44
3. Psalm 139:13–16
4. Ephesians 2:8
5. Hebrews 11:1
6. Matthew 13:31
7. Mark 4:26–27 NASB
8. 1 Corinthians 3:6
9. Ghulam Masih Naaman, *My Grace is Sufficient for You: A Testimony from Pakistan* (The Good Way, 2003), http://www.the-good-way.com/eng/books/.
10. Luke 12: 50–53
11. 2 Peter 3:9
12. Matthew 2:16
13. Matthew 2:18
14. Al-Jazeerah has since removed the interview and details, but it remains in other location on the Internet including https://www.youtube.com/watch?v=CDzDSYHbTOM/.
15. 1 Peter 4:14
16. Matthew 28:20 NASB
17. John 16:33
18. 1 John 3:1
19. 1 Peter 1:3
20. Galatians 2:20

Chapter 12: Knowing Christ with Us

1. John 16:33
2. Matthew 28:20
3. Matthew 28:16
4. Luke 24:50
5. Luke 24:51
6. John 14:18
7. John 14:17
8. Luke 24:52
9. 2 Corinthians 4:6–7
10. 1 Corinthians 6:19
11. Luke 24:49
12. Galatians 5:22–23
13. Ephesians 3:16
14. Ephesians 3:17
15. Ephesians 3:19
16. See http://en.wikipedia.org/wiki/Nine_Lessons_and_Carols.
17. John 15:13 NIV
18. Matthew 25:21
19. Matthew 16:25 NIV
20. 1 John 1:5
21. 1 John 3:1
22. Matthew 28:20
23. Romans 8:38–39
24. Romans 8:37

Final Thoughts: Deeply Grateful

1. Luke 22:24
2. John 11:35
3. Luke 19:41
4. John 15:20
5. Philippians 3:10 NASB

ACKNOWLEDGMENTS

I want to thank all those who shared their thoughts and reflections for inclusion in this work. I know that condensing significant, powerful, and often heartbreaking experiences into a few words is incredibly difficult. Thank you! I'm grateful, also, to those who wanted to contribute but were unable to find the words. Our conversations encouraged me to write what they could not say. I hope I've come close.

I'd also like to thank all those who've prayed for me through the writing, just as you prayed for me while I lived in a dangerous place. You are each a gift to my life, and I thank God for you.

My thanks go to Judy Dunagan for encouraging me to write this book and to Moody Publishers for believing in the project. Thank you, Michele Forrider, for inviting me to Moody Bible Institute to share these truths with college students. Without your work, this book wouldn't have been written! My thanks also to Janis Backing who so wonderfully plans, welcomes, and cares for me each time I come to Moody.

Finally, thank You, Jesus, for inviting me to walk with You in a dangerous place and for leading me so deep into Your heart. Please, hold my hand always!

MORE FROM
KATE McCORD

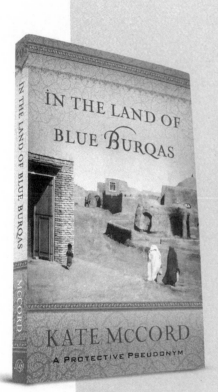

In the Land of Blue Burqas is based on the real dangers and firsthand accounts from the author's experiences living in Afghanistan. It reveals the splendor of Christ, the desire of human hearts, and the precious instances where the two meet.

MORE FROM
KATE McCORD

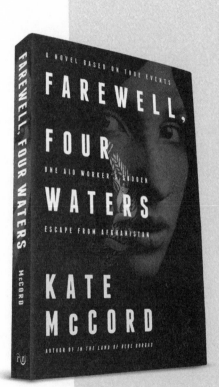

Farewell, Four Waters is a novel based on actual events the author and other aid workers faced in Afghanistan in 2008. See through their eyes the dangers faced globally even today.

MOODY
Publishers™

From the Word to Life

the **LAND** and the **BOOK**
with Dr. Charlie Dyer

Dr. Charlie Dyer provides biblical insight into the complex tapestry of people and events that make up Israel and the Middle East. Each week he presents an in-depth look at biblical, historical, archeological, and prophetic events and their relevance for today.

www.thelandandthebook.org

MOODY
Radio™

From the Word **to Life**